Wizoo Guide

Logic Audio Macintosh 4

Dave Bellingham

Logic AUDIO

Logic Audio Macintosh 4

Imprint

Publisher Peter Gorges

Author Dave Bellingham

Printed in Belgium
ISBN 3-927954-50-0

Proofreading Edwin Hettinger
Layout and typesetting Uwe Senkler, Hamburg
Cover design design-box, Ravensburg
Printed by Continental Printing/EGRA Grafik GmbH

Welcome …

This Wizoo Guide to Emagic's Logic Audio for Macintosh was written for those of you who are relatively new to the program and those who would like to fully take advantage of the audio facilities in version 4.

The guide also covers the selection of suitable hardware so that you can make music, not sit for hours screaming at your Macintosh and talking to support techs on the phone.

The guide is *not* intended as a manual replacement, but rather as an adjunct to it which covers the practical use of the audio functions of the software with loads of practical examples, uses and explanations *in a ›musical‹ context,* both in the pages and on the accompanying CD-ROM.

It is strongly recommended that you are in front of your computer with your version of Logic Audio booted up and ready to go as many of the explanations are best understood if you can see and hear what's going on.

Alternately, you can browse the CD and check out the examples chapter by chapter.

Are you ready to have some fun?

Batteries to power, turbines to speed…

Dave Bellingham

Table of Contents

1 Basic Concepts

This chapter covers some basic things you should know about Logic Audio for Mac Os (from here on, referred to as LAM) and my general approach to this guide. Also included at the end of the chapter is a rundown on the various flavors of LAM—Platinum, Gold, Silver—to help you decide which version is best for you. I know that you're probably ready to go *now* and that the last thing you want is some windbag rambling on but I promise that you will be making more *effective* and *efficient* use of LAM in just a few hours.

Book Updates

The guide is based on LAM 4.0. Should there be any functional changes which supercede the information contained in the book, you will find corrections at

`http://www.wizoo.com/docs/english/bookservice/lam.htm`

About LAM 4

For anyone who's upgraded from a previous version, here's an overview of the main new features:

Changed Local Menus

When you first boot V 4 of LAM, you will notice quite a few cosmetic changes, not the least of which is fewer local menu options on the individual edit windows. This has been supplanted by the more obvious use of the main menu bar for many setup functions and a separate Audio menu where you'll, not surprisingly, find audio-related functions.

Improved Speed

The one *monster* thing is that the software has been optimized big time with this version, affording a huge boost in performance. This means more tracks and Fx, tighter MIDI timing, faster screen redraws and faster processing of audio than you were previously getting out of your Macintosh, and you've gotta love that!

24-Bit/96-kHz Support

LAM Platinum allows you to switch between different sample rates up to 96 kHz with 24-bit resolution, provided you have the appropriate hardware.

► There are hundreds of other little (and big) changes that you'll discover as you work with version 4, but these are less significant from a general operational standpoint.

Before I Start

The LAM series sequencers are complex. You will need to practice a lot before you master them ... Grasshopper.

I want to familiarize you with LAM's range of funky audio options, show you some cool tricks you may not have thought of, and to assist you in developing some good habits and working practices.

The point of telling you this?—*read the manual!* (not right now ... but soon)

There are some things that won't be covered and this is where the manual comes in handy ... read it at some stage over the next few weeks.

LAM Is Customizable

LAM can be customized in hundreds of ways to make it *your* sequencer. Outside of customizing your Environment, you can set up your edit windows—and therefore your method of working—through the use of Screensets, changing the Key Commands (computer keyboard shortcuts) to keys that make sense to you and much more. This inherent flexibility is a wonderful thing, but for many users new to the program, it may not seem ›Logic‹-al at all.

In my opinion, LAM is much more a program for lateral thinkers, but ›Lateral Audio‹ would have been a really crappy name.

The point of telling you all this? In the context of the guide's accompanying CD-ROM you will be dealing with *my* customized environments, so my apologies in advance if your head doesn't work this way.

Someone's Done It Already

There are tens of thousands of LOGIC users out there.

If you're not on the Internet, put down this book, go to the bank, withdraw some cash and buy yourself a modem.

If you already have a modem, there's a vast resource available of ready-made environments and more which can be used directly in your setup for hundreds of different devices and situations.

There is a User's Group where you can ask ›dumb‹ questions without fear of abuse and—here and elsewhere—you can download patches, updates and bugfixes as soon as they're available.

This treasure chest of ›freebies‹ has gotta be taken advantage of. If some kind soul has dedicated their time and effort for nothing but good karma points, then your download will assist them on their path to enlightenment. When you're a LAM guru, you can repay the favor by uploading an environment, transformer or by offering some assistance to another user who's where you may be now.

Makes you feel all ›warm and fuzzy,‹ doesn't it?

About the CD-ROM

The CD-ROM which accompanies the guide is chock full of useful stuff (close to 500 MB worth, in fact!) which will assist you in getting the most out of the text and LAM itself.

My intention was to provide you with a ›one stop shop‹ which offered more utilities, Emagic drivers and demo versions than you could possibly imagine in one place. Additionally, there is a vast amount of documentation on disc. And for online users ... even more info at my Logic FAQ page `http://www.ozemail.com.au/~oscwilde`

Please thoroughly read the `readme` file found in the root folder of the CD-ROM. It contains the latest info, setup tips and all known bugs and issues which may be relevant to your system.

Browsing the Disc

Simply double-click on the `Default.htm` document in the root folder of the CD. This will launch your preferred Internet browser.

Copying the Song Files

NB: The song files, particularly those with automation examples, may lag on playback on your system. Read the section on ›Latency‹ (see page 78) for more info.

For the song files, you will need to copy both the `Songs` folder and the `Audio` folder to the root directory of your hard disk by highlighting the folders with your mouse and drag 'n dropping 'em on your hard disk icon on the desktop. Throughout the book, there are references to example song files which can be opened by launching LAM and selecting the designated file from the hard disk or by double-clicking directly on the song file name within the `Songs` folder. This will open LAM and load the song file.

Most examples can be listened to as audio files (where applicable) directly from the browser, so you have a choice of which way you'd like to go about it.

Song files are indicated as in the following example:

- Filename—A description of the file

Plug-ins and Shareware

Also included—heaps of third-party VST plug-ins for you to try out, plus a number of Emagic demos and drivers, a couple of extremely useful (essential, I feel) shareware music utilities and a copy of Adobe's Acrobat reader which will allow you to read some documents on the CD which are saved in PDF format.

All in all, I'm positive you will find the CD-ROM extremely useful and very easy to get around.

CD-ROM Table of Contents

There is a *full* table of contents on the CD which can be viewed once the browser is launched. Just click on ›Table of Contents‹ in the left-hand frame. From the TOC window, you can view or execute files by clicking on any link that is of interest. Alternately, you can open the SimpleText document called `Table of Contents` which is found in the root directory of the CD.

Folder	Contents
`3rd party`	Contains dozens of demo versions of third-party application software and plug-ins plus multimedia demos, descriptions and application guides. Also a huge amount of documentation which will assist you in understanding how to use the plug-ins, installation tips and tricks and much more. Save yourself the time, effort and expense of downloading *hundreds* of megabytes of data over the Internet.
`acroread`	Acrobat reader from Adobe for browsing PDF documents featured on the CD
`audio`	Audio files used for the book examples will give you plenty of material to experiment with plus a great insight into how things work in LAM. These can be auditioned via your Internet browser or within LAM.

docs	Hypertext documentation for the guide and the latest listings (and hypertext links for anyone online) to hardware manufacturers. This is *the* place to look if you're troubleshooting.
emagic	Demo versions of Emagic software, including SoundDiver, LAM 3.5, HearMaster *plus* Audiowerk and Unitor8 drivers and more for you to check out.
share	A useful and essential collection of shareware audio applications
songs	Song files used in the book examples. These will allow you to try your *own* settings and will assist in quickly learning how to make the most of LAM

► Some of the samples featured on the CD are from the Wizoo CD-ROMS ›Hamburg Loopz‹ and ›Lofi Junkiez‹ available in WAV/AIFF format, for use with LAM.

Which Metal Should I Choose?

Great question—glad you asked.

The choice of which version of LAM is best suited to your needs is pretty simple really. It comes down to these basic factors.

- Money—as in how much of it do you have?
- Facilities you actually *need*, now and in the foreseeable future

► A bonus for anyone who purchases Silver or Gold is that Emagic and their distributors are happy to upgrade your version should you need the additional features of higher versions at some point in the future. This upgrade is generally around the cost difference between the two products. Check with your local distributor.

Platinum

The flagship—for Pro and Semi-Pro users. Vast creative options in the form of Fx and general audio handling facilities:

- Supports up to 64 tracks of audio (128 with multiple hardware)
- 24-bit/96k-Hz hardware supported
- Full scoring features
- Full blown environment capabilities
- 4 × parametric EQ per channel/track
- Loads of internal Fx algorithms (40, in fact) including: Chorus, Ensemble, Flanger, Phaser, Compressor, Reverb, Spectral Gate, Expander, Delay, Pitch Shifter, Enveloper & Noise Gate, Autofilter, Bitcrusher, Distortion, Overdrive and a range of EQ options.
- Up to sixteen Fx busses for major routing possibilities,
- Sophisticated synchronization facilities and much more.

Gold

Pretty much as above, but limited as follows:

- Only 32 tracks of audio (64 with additional AV)
- Eight Fx busses
- Does not support 24-bit hardware
- Limited number of plug-in effects—does *not* include Autofilter, Spectral Gate, Enveloper, Phaser, ›Platinum‹ versions of Reverb & Compressor or Enverb or Direction Mixer.

Most users will be more than happy with Gold, including many Pros. The primary differences between it and Platinum are: less hardware support (for more audio tracks—although 32 is usually enough for most situations), and the additional Fx options offered by Platinum.

Silver

- Up to 24 tracks of audio
- Four Fx busses
- Fourteen internal Fx
- Older version of Time and Pitch Machine
- Reduced environment and scoring facilities
- Less hardware support, no simultaneous use of Macintosh Av and other hardware
- Fewer Digital Factory options
- Very limited synchronization—forget it for SMPTE

If your audio needs don't extend too far, you're on a budget and really only want to knock about at home, or are primarily interested in sequencing rather than hardcore audio manipulation, then Silver is a good choice.

If, on the other hand, you have any need for higher quality Fx algorithms (primary vocal reverbs etc.) or need to radically alter tracks (remixers take note), then go directly to either Gold or Platinum. You will probably find Silver lacks the range and quality of Fx for your processing needs.

► NB: For maximum tracks, bussing etc. your Macintosh's hard disk subsystem, memory subsystem etc. needs to be configured properly and well specified.

All Versions Feature

- 960 ppqn resolution
- Virtually unlimited MIDI tracks
- Extensive quantization options
- Stereo sample editor
- Support for VST, Audiosuite, and Premiere plug-ins
- Copy protection: The top two use a dongle, Silver uses a key-disk.

2 What Sort of Macintosh Should I Use for LAM?

For real-time applications such as LAM, it's essential that you select the right hardware and software for your system and configure these components properly. This doesn't mean that only a high-end Macintosh and the most expensive, sophisticated peripheral hardware will give you wicked results with LAM, but you should be aware of where you can cut corners and where you can't.

As a Macintosh user, you won't encounter the kind of headaches that Windows PC users have to deal with when selecting the best computer for LAM simply because the Macintosh ships as an all-inclusive package.

Compared with previous versions, Emagic upped the ante for LAM 4.

- PPC version: Apple Macintosh with PowerPC processor, 120 MHz and 64 MB RAM, Mac OS 7.1 (and higher)
- For 68k version: 68040 processor, Digidesign Nubus hardware
- Recommended: Apple Macintosh G3 128 MB RAM, Mac OS 8.1 (and higher)

What this means in practical terms is that LAM will run OK on anything but an ancient (relatively speaking, of course) PowerMacintosh model, but it will take a very recent Macintosh (did someone say G3?) to make the most of the program.

I don't recommend the use of the 68k version as these Macintoshs simply lack the grunt for realtime DSP. If you're only into sequencing, and maybe a couple of audio tracks, then they may do the trick for you.

Before we dive in...

A bit of advice: If you're no expert on computers, it's worthwhile going to a computer music specialist (i. e. a music store) rather than the local Apple dealer to ask hardware questions. If you've got a friend who's ›really into computers‹ or a ›bit of a Mac guru,‹ you *may* rely on their advice, but more often than not, these ›wizards‹ are actually hip with running Photoshop or Director, *not* recording digital audio and running a MIDI recording studio.

Music stores are the only people who can sell LAM, they know what the software requires to run and, in many cases, will set it up for you (for a small charge or gratis) when you buy the program. If you buy your Macintosh from them as well, it may cost a little extra, but you'll be able to get the support you may need with LAM and any other audio/music programs you run in the future.

Now onto the bits ...

Central Processing Unit (CPU)

The CPU of the computer is the ›brain‹ of the machine ... and is the component primarily responsible for your system's performance.

As a general rule of thumb, the newer the processor type, the higher the computing performance. In terms of LAM performance, this means primarily—more EQs and effects. Macintosh computers have, over the years, featured three major processor families.

68k Processors

You might be familiar with the family of so-called ›68k‹ processors from way back in the Atari or Amiga days. Although a Macintosh equipped with a 68k processor hasn't been released since 1995, you can still find models such as the Quadra or LC on the second-hand market.

A word to the wise: The cost of upgrading a 68k Macintosh to the level of a PowerMacintosh is unacceptable in price/performance terms. Another factor is that any 040-based machine with a PPC upgrade card in it will *not* work with Mac Os 8.6. My recommendation on buying a used 68k Macintosh for LAM: Don't!

PowerMac Processors

The processors of the PowerMacintosh family (from here on referred to as ›PPC‹) found in Power Macintosh models were the Apple standard from 1995 to 1997.

From early 1998, the G3 became the new fair-haired boy of the bunch, but more on that in a moment ...

Just to make things difficult, you should be aware that there are different chip generations within the PowerMacintosh family. The early Power Macintosh computers equipped with a PPC 601 CPU are too slow for *effective* use with LAM 4. The *minimum* (i. e. slowest performance) chip that I can recommend is the PPC 603e processor—the middle generation of the PowerMacintosh chips.

The PPC 604 and the PPC 604e are the later PowerMacintosh generations, where the latter is a particularly promising proposition for LAM because it excels at floating point calculations, an operation which LAM has a penchant for.

If you run into third-party processor cards labeled ›604r‹ or ›Mach 5‹ don't be confused: These are simply slightly improved versions of the 604e.

The last of the Power Macintosh models equipped with a 604e processor can be had cheaply on the second-hand market ... and while the sexy new ›blue and white‹ G3s are appealing, if you're *really* short of cash, consider a 604e processor-based Macintosh. Better yet, look for a second-hand Macintosh built around the ...

G3 Processors

From the end of 1997/early '98, all new Macintoshs feature the G3 processor. G3 stands for Generation 3. Its formal nomenclature is PPC 750. Although the 750 still carries the PowerMacintosh prefix, it features a number of technical improvements that put it way in front of the older processor generation (see ›Cache‹ on page 25).

The bottom line is that the performance of the G3 processor is better than its PowerMacintosh predecessors. If you're looking at buying a new box specifically for use with LAM, definitely go for one of the ›blue and white‹ G3 processor-equipped Macintoshs.

Clock

Even if you're a computer newbie, you've probably heard that the clock rate of a computer is a crucial factor in the performance of the machine. However, you may not be familiar with the fact that there is a difference between CPU and system bus clock:

- **CPU clock:** This is the frequency at which the CPU can process commands. For Apple computers, this value is indicated after the slash in a model designation, for example PM 7300/166 indicates a CPU clock of 166 MHz.

  For LAM 4 PPC, your box will need (at least) a CPU clock rate of 120 MHz. The lowest model available on the G3 computer scale features a 233 MHz clock, the top dog 450 MHz. G3 computers featuring speeds above 450 MHz and the next-generation of Macintosh processors called ... the G4 (rather inspired, I thought) ... which will probably start at this clock rate are on their way.
- **System bus clock:** This value indicates how fast the CPU can exchange data with other components such as the RAM and Level 2 Cache (see page 25). Like a Ferrari loaded with a Honda Civic transmission, an extremely high CPU clock won't do much good if the system bus clock is too low—the CPU has to idle while it waits for the other computer components to respond. The Power Macintosh range features system busses of up to 50 MHz; at 66 MHz, the first G3 system busses were somewhat

improved and the ›blue and white‹ G3 Macintoshs have taken this up to a whopping 100 MHz!

CPU and system bus clock can have almost as much bearing on overall computing performance as the actual type of CPU you choose. For LAM, this means more software EQs and effects that you can run simultaneously, so …

When you're looking for a LAM 4 computer, try scoring a box that features a CPU clock of at least 120 MHz and a PPC 603e (or preferably G3)—nothing less will do. This drastically reduces potential second-hand choices. The system bus clock specification comes into play when you're comparing different computer generations (Power Macintosh versus G3) or considering a processor upgrade (see page 45).

► It's worth noting that Power Macintoshs with twice the CPU clock won't necessarily deliver twice the performance. Due to similarly low system bus stats, the boost in performance is often closer to 70%. You should keep this in mind when you're shopping—is the performance that you're actually getting worth what you have to pay for it?

► With the blue and white G3s, the increase in the system bus speed represents a significant increase in the speed of communication between components. PCI cards, hard disks and memory can all ›talk‹ to each other up to 50% faster than an earlier G3 running at the same clock speed.

RAM

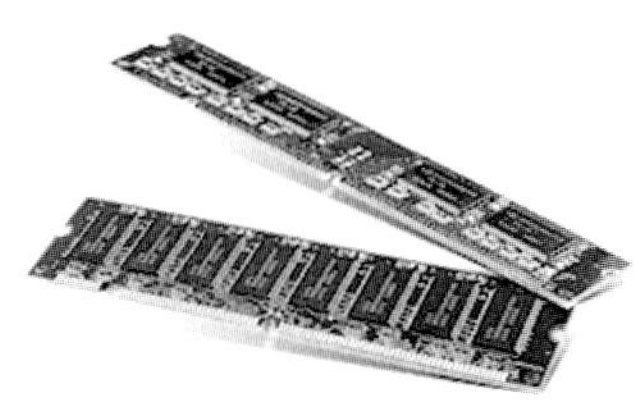

RAM is the ›volatile‹ memory of the computer, and is where your applications actually do their stuff. You'll find that you can access data residing in RAM substantially faster than executing read and write operations on the hard disk.

For LAM—in addition to the RAM's standard functions—RAM is particularly valuable as a fast buffer for data. During audio playback, data is temporarily ›parked‹ in the RAM to compensate for data flow fluctuations between the disk and CPU.

When you're buying a computer, ensure that not all of the computer's RAM slots have small memory modules plugged into them. With a couple of free slots, you'll have plenty of leeway for subsequent expansions and you won't have to relegate your old chips to recycling Hell.

► Emagic specifies a minimum RAM requirement of 48 MB reserved for LAM. To meet this prerequisite—especially when you consider the increasingly resource-hungry Mac OS versions that you may want to work with in the future (and you're probably using now)—you shouldn't mess around with anything less than 64 MB... better yet, go directly to 128.

If you find that, at some point, you want to expand the RAM, the different computer models require different types of RAM:

- The majority of Power Macintosh computers work with 168-pin 5-V DIMMs.
- The Power Macintosh 4400 requires 3.3-V EDO DIMMS.
- The first generation of Power Macintosh models (PM 6100, 7100 and 8100) work with 72-pin PS/2 modules.
- G3 computers use faster SDRAM DIMM modules.
- Blue and white G3s use ›standard‹ 3.3-V PC100 SDRAM modules, like those used in Windows PCs. This is a great thing because due to the large market for this type of memory, SDRAM chips are not only plentiful, but are also cheap.

DIMM modules can be plugged in individually, but this puts a serious damper on speed. Make sure you buy DIMMs in identical pairs. Plug one component into an A slot and the other into the B slot with an identical number (as labeled on the board). This is the only way you can be sure that the RAM delivers the speed it's capable of. The blue and white G3s do not require matching memory pairs.

At approximately 60 ns (nanoseconds—thousandths of a second), the memory modules in the Power Macintoshs are relatively sluggish. The SDRAM in the G3 computers isn't much more expensive, but running at 10 ns, is substantially faster. Whereas the other memory types have a maximum size of 64 or 128 MB, G3 SDRAM is available as a 256 MB module, which obviously means that G3 computers are well ahead of the pack in terms of RAM expansion options.

The blue and white G3s can take up to 1 gigabyte of RAM and as PC100 RAM runs on a *much* faster bus, they frankly kick ass!

► If you own a blue and white G3, ensure that any memory you add to your machine is PC100-compliant RAM. Other slower (and cheaper) memory modules (66 MHz) will fit the slots and will work but won't give you all of the possible performance. This isn't major, as we're talking nanoseconds here, but I thought you should know to avoid being ripped off by a less than reputable dealer, who often remark chips.

Realtime audio applications like LAM have an insatiable appetite for ›real‹ RAM. LAM won't settle for imitations—so programs that feed portions of the hard disk to the computer as virtual memory (e. g. Connectix RAM Doubler) are *not* suitable.

Cache

The term ›cache‹ in computer lingo describes a generally small but very fast type of memory buffer.

The processor loads most commands and data to this buffer and whenever it needs to access to these, it can retrieve them much faster than it could from the much slower main system RAM.

LAM transports heaps of sample data during audio recording and playback. This data is routed via the Level 2 cache, which usually resides on the main board. Generally, there are three options available:

- **Modules**: Most Power Macintoshs feature the best solution—slots for the Level 2 Cache. Here you can plug in a suitable memory module; generally these come in 256 kB, 512 kB and 1,024 kB versions. You should be aware that these modules are much faster than normal RAM, which of course translates to a bigger hole in your wallet. LAM will do with at least a 256 kB Level 2 Cache; like most applications.

► For most older Macintoshs, if you're considering upgrading the Level 2 Cache to more than 256 kB, be aware that you'll be wasting your bucks. However, in accelerated older models and the new G3 Macintoshs, cache makes a difference. The larger the gap between CPU and bus clock rate, the higher the influence of Level 2 cache.

- **Soldered**: In a few Power Macintosh models, the Level 2 Cache is hard-wired to the board. The good news is that LAM doesn't mind, the bad news is that if these memory models break down or are too slow for an upgrade, you're screwed.
- **None**: If your computer is equipped with neither a soldered Level 2 Cache nor the requisite slots—which is the case with several Powerbooks—forget about running LAM on it.

The latest Macintosh models feature Level 2 Cache innovations that can boost LAM performance:

- **Inline Cache**: Here the Level 2 cache is packed up and moved from the mainboard over to the processor card. The bonus here is that the processor can communicate with this form of cache at a far higher clock rate than via the system bus.

► The Power Macintoshs 8600 and 9600 featuring 250 MHz and higher CPUs are equipped with a 1,024 kB inline cache that is accessed at double the system bus clock (100 MHz).

◆ **Backside Cache**: In G3 computers, the inline cache concept is taken a step further. These feature a dedicated bus for data transfer between the processor and the cache (max. 1,024 kB), which also resides on the processor card. Most G3 models (including the blue and white ones) use half the CPU clock speed as the transfer rate on this bus. Some G3 upgrade cards available from third-party vendors address the Backside Cache at the full CPU clock rate.

► The blue and white G3s all feature a 1,024 kB backside cache (except the 300 MHz model, which has 512 kB) running at half the processor clock speed (e.g. 150 MHz on G3/300, 200 MHz on G3/400).

In a conventional Level 2 Cache, an upgrade of the 256 kB minimum requirement won't do much good. If the processor is geared to exploit the substantially more effective Inline or, even better, the Backside Cache, you can appreciably increase the performance via a cache upgrade (for example from 512 to 1,024 kB).

Expansion Slot Formats

Many Macintosh models seem pretty well-loaded at first glance, but as computer-based musicians (a.k.a.—gear sluts) we all find ourselves lusting after newer and/or more toys after a while—another graphics card, a faster SCSI controller or a more powerful audio card. Mmmmmm ...

In Macland, there are, or more accurately *were*, two slot formats to plug hardware into:

◆ **Nubus**: The first Macintosh generations with PPC processors (PowerMacintosh 6100, 7100, 8100) were based on mainboards with Nubus slots. As a potential LAM user, avoid these computers like the plague. Why? Because up-to-date Macintosh audio cards—and just about every other expansion possibility—are only available in PCI format.

- **PCI**: With the Power Macintosh 9500, Apple introduced the PCI slot format and has since equipped virtually all of the company's computers with this type of slot.

Apple's willingness to commit to the format has made the PCI bus the standard in the Windows PC world as well. Macintosh users benefit from this development—some PCI cards that were developed for the ›mainstream PC market‹ are also available cheaply for PCI Macintoshs.

Slap in an audio card, an additional graphics card and a SCSI controller—presto—there go three PCI slots up in smoke. We're not talking decadent luxury here—this is all standard equipment. Macintosh models featuring three PCI slots are pretty much the norm in the mid-range market and should do the trick for most users. Don't buy a baby Macintosh with just one PCI slot; you'll limit your choices too much with LAM.

Although the computer industry claims that PCI is a ›platform-independent‹ standard, the cold hard truth is that software or hardware incompatibilities often cause major headaches when porting PCI card drivers to the Macintosh. Here's where a basic mistrust of technology, human nature, or both, come in handy. You should never order a new PCI component for the Macintosh on good faith—wait for your local dealer to fit the product in a demo computer and see for yourself if the thing works the way it should.

Peripheral Interfaces

On most Macintoshs, two ›standards‹—E-IDE and SCSI—facilitate data exchange between the CPU and peripheral devices such as hard disks or CD-ROM drives.

► On the new ›blue and white‹ G3 Macintoshs, SCSI has been put out to pasture (except on some 400 MHz and higher models—even here it's via a plug-in PCI card) and has been supplanted by Firewire (read the section entitled ›Next Generation Peripheral Interfaces‹ from page 32 onwards for more info about this).

Different combinations are available depending on the Macintosh model, so if you want to connect two E-IDE disks to a single E-IDE bus (Master/Slave) the same way your Windows PC owning friends do, you'll have to go for the second generation of G3 models.

E-IDE

Apple introduced the first E-IDE interface for Macintosh in 1994 on the Performa 630. Since then, the number of Macintosh models with one or two internal E-IDE busses has been on the rise. This includes the blue and white G3s.

When you run across a single E-IDE bus, it's always connected to the internal program hard disk. Often, people talk about ›IDE‹—the ›E‹ falls by the wayside. In most cases, they are referring to E-IDE, not its antiquated granddad. If a computer features a second internal E-IDE bus, it usually communicates with the internal E-IDE-compatible CD-ROM drive (ATAPI). E-IDE hard disks are generally cheaper than SCSI drives, but unfortunately, they're generally slower, although Ultra-ATA drives are pretty quick and compete with Ultra SCSI (up to 40 MB/sec).

SCSI

Once the preserve of the Apple faithful, the SCSI bus is now commonplace on Windows PCs. Compared with E-IDE, SCSI lets you connect up to seven or even fourteen devices to a single bus and run these simultaneously.

Since the Macintosh Plus saw the light of day (1986), every Macintosh has featured an external SCSI interface (with two exceptions—the iMac, see page 47, and the blue and white G3).

The first generation of PCI Macintoshs (7500, 7600, 8500, 8600, 9500 and 9600) featured—in addition to the external standard SCSI—an internal Fast SCSI 2 bus. The second generation, namely the beige G3s, used external standard SCSI plus two internal IDE busses, whereas the third generation Macintoshs (blue and white G3s) are limited to only one IDE internally, but finally feature a DMA busmaster function.

The internal program hard disk isn't picky, it doesn't care if it has to deal with an E-IDE or a SCSI bus. However, audio hard disks are an entirely different story—to cope with the huge amount of data throughput, you should definitely go for a fast SCSI bus for the best results. In the blue and white G3s, the internal IDE hard disk is an ATA device and is certainly fast enough for hard disk recording. My recommendation, however, is to take a look at Firewire (page 32).

The advantages of the SCSI bus include:

- Adding a new hard drive (or other peripheral) is (theoretically) as simple as setting a number (SCSI ID), connecting it, and turning on your Macintosh.
- Up to fourteen devices can be chained off a single SCSI controller card.
- SCSI doesn't have the CPU overhead of IDE so you will get faster performance and more tracks (in general). Be aware that SCSI is only as fast as the weakest link in the SCSI chain, so there's no point in having either a high spec drive or high spec SCSI adapter if the other component(s) can't also run at that sort of speed.

If you decide on a Scsi system, there are several different Scsi ›flavors‹ to choose from. These determine—among other factors—the peak speed of the controller and the maximum number of Scsi devices that it can handle:

- Standard: a.k.a. ›Narrow,‹ 8-bit bus width, speed of 5 MHz, 5 Mb/sec
- Fast: 8-bit bus width, speed of 10 MHz, 10 Mb/sec
- Ultra: 8-bit bus width, speed of 20 MHz, 20 Mb/sec
- Wide: 16-bit bus width, speed of 10 MHz, 20 Mb/sec
- Ultra Wide: 16- to 64-bit bus width, speed of 20 MHz, 40 Mb/sec
- Ultra 2: 16- to 64-bit bus width, speed of 40 MHz, 80 Mb/sec

Nb: The data throughput values (Mb/sec) refer to ›Burst Speed‹ which, in the real world, is not that relevant.

Some Pros and Cons of Scsi

- If you decide to go for a Scsi-based system, be aware that some Scsi interfaces can introduce noise into your system and therefore into your recordings.
- Be extremely careful when shopping for your Scsi interface and specify that you want to use it for hard disk recording. This way, if the vendor gives you bad advice you can return or exchange it if you need to. Legally, this is called ›duty of care‹ and is found in most local Trade or Business Practices Acts.
- In addition to higher performance, Scsi has other advantages, particularly in studio environments. Many samplers can now swap audio data with computers via Scsi; data transfer between Macintosh and Windows Pcs is also made much easier via Scsi.
- Getting a Scsi system up and running (and continuing to run) can be something of a black art, with many users falling prey to problems with termination settings, device Ids etc. Take a look at the Cd-Rom troubleshooting documentation for symptoms and cures.

With a Fast Scsi controller, which is twice as fast as Scsi 1, and a decent hard disk, you shouldn't have any problems playing 24 audio tracks. Most Lam users will be safe with this type of controller (Scsi 2 or ›Fast‹).

Next Generation Peripheral Interfaces

The new ›blue and white‹ G3 Macintoshs introduce two new peripheral interfaces, namely USB and Firewire. Each interface promises simple ›plug n play‹ operation and reasonable to extremely fast data throughput. Both are serial interfaces and allow the connection of not only storage devices (hard disks, CD Recorders etc.), but also other peripherals such as digital cameras, scanners and MIDI interfaces.

Firewire

Fitted as standard equipment on the ›blue and white‹ G3 Macintoshs are two Firewire ports. This serial protocol delivers throughput of approx. 150 MB/sec, supports up to 63 devices per bus, has automatic ID configuration, self-termination and the option of connecting devices while the system is up and running. These features should put an end to the voodoo required to keep a SCSI sytem running flawlessly, but like all good things ... we'll just have to wait for more peripherals to start appearing. At the time of writing, a number of hard disk manufacturers had finally committed to actually building Firewire drives. Hopefully, all of you new G3 owners (myself included) should have a wide choice by the time you read this.

USB (Universal Serial Bus)

USB delivers data throughput of up to 12 MBit/sec (theoretically) and can support up to 127 devices, including the Macintosh keyboard/mouse, ZIP (and other) drives, and MIDI interfaces. This last point is particularly important because this new breed of G3s has sacrificed the Macintosh serial ports, so your existing MIDI interface will *not* be able to be used on these new Macintoshs without an adapter (read more on this ›Serial Port Adapter solutions for the Blue G3‹ on page 74).

USB is presently unsupported by any device (i.e. a hard disk) to make it useful for hard disk recording/playback. All current devices (Zip drives etc.) are too slow, and this lack of speed seems to be a problem for the bus as a whole. Maybe time will change this?

If you own a new ›blue‹ G3, I would have to recommend that you forget about Usb and go directly to a Firewire hard disk which will give you (theoretically) vastly superior performance. Use the Usb port for your Midi interface and other less demanding peripherals.

Usb has the following pluses:

- It is ›hot-swappable,‹ which means that you can plug/unplug peripherals while the computer is running.
- You can use your Usb devices on both Mac Os and Windows computers—if you have an appropriate driver for both platforms—making the swapping of data easy. Most new Windows Pcs (Pentium II and up) come with Usb ports as standard.

Scsi on the Blue and White G3

If you have existing Scsi drives and peripherals you'd like to take with you, the following Pci Scsi cards are available from these suppliers for the G3 (blue/white):

- Apple (only via built-to-order option)
- Adaptec, PowerDomain—`http://www.adaptec.com/`
- Advansys, Asb—`http://www.advansys.com/`
- Atto, ExpressPci—`http://www.atotech.com/`
- Formac, ProRaid—`http://www.formac.de/`
- Initio, Miles Scsi cards—`http://www.initio.com/`
- Orange Micro, Grappler Scsi—`http://www.orangemicro.com/`

► It's strongly recommended that you install the current firmware (for the Pci Scsi card) as many older cards had to be adapted to the new blue G3. Also very important is that the latest version of the appropriate hard disk driver is used.

► A USB to SCSI converter is *not* recommended for musicians because the data throughput rate (less than 1 MB/sec) is too low.

All about Hard Disks

Hard drives (a.k.a. hard disks) are an essential component in the success of your recording experience with Logic Audio.

You'll need at least one large hard disk with an access time of 10 ms (milliseconds) or faster for recording and playback of multiple audio tracks. Read carefully through the following topics for loads more info on access time and other factors in the choice of hard disks.

It is strongly recommended that you use a separate ›working‹ hard disk for your audio files and another which contains your applications and operating system as this significantly reduces the risk of file corruptions to your system files.

Also take into account the fact that the CPU and other components covered in this chapter also have a major part to play here as a faster machine will speed up the disk transfer rate, so installing a super-fast drive into a slow Macintosh won't do the trick. You need to go the whole hog and have a fast CPU, cache, memory, busses and hard disk(s).

Seek Time

The amount of time it takes the actuator arm to move the read/write head between tracks is called seek time. As most hard disks have around 3,000 tracks on each side of a 3.5-inch platter, the actuator arm might move just one track or up to 2,999 tracks.

Seek time is measured in milliseconds (ms) with times between adjacent tracks being as short as 2 ms, and seeks from one side of the disk to the other taking about 20 ms. From this, an ›average seek time‹ is defined with most drives falling in the 8 to 14 ms range.

If you hear a reference to a drive like ›it's got a 14 millisecond seek‹ then you're not getting the whole picture. Use seek time as only *one* of many specs when evaluating a drive.

Data Transfer Rates

After positioning the read/write head when a disk first ›spins-up,‹ the drive is ready to read or write data from/to the disk. In either case, a data transfer of some sort will happen between the disk and the CPU. The faster this data transfer, the less time you have to wait for your apps to do their stuff.

The data transfer rate depends on the following two factors:

- the disk transfer rate, or how fast data is passed from the disk to the peripheral interface (a.k.a. hard disk controller)
- the host transfer rate, or how fast the controller passes data to the computer's CPU.

The data transfer rate is measured in megabytes per second (MB/sec).

Data Throughput

Data throughput rate is a measurement reflecting both data access time (seek) and data transfer rate i. e.—the total amount of data that the CPU can access in a given amount of time. As such, it is a good indicator of the general performance of the drive, *but* data throughput measurements also reflect the speed of the host computer, and this should be taken into account.

The bottom line is that, provided the rest of your system components can process the data as quickly as the hard drive can read or write it, data throughput is the best spec to check out when evaluating a hard disks performance.

For digital audio data transfers, use the following data throughput equation:

1 minute = 60 seconds = 5 MB of data

NB: The figures on any spec sheets referring to Data Throughput would need to have been tested on an actual Macintosh. If you can, find out what processor speed, RAM amount etc. were used to arrive at the manufacturer's results. Obviously, a faster Macintosh should (theoretically) make this figure higher.

1 second = 5 MB of data divided by 60 seconds = approx. 83.3 kB of data per second

So, using the formula above, if you want LAM to play back 16 audio tracks simultaneously you'll need a data throughput rate of at least 16 × 83.3 kB = approx. 1.3 MB/sec.

To be safe, you should look at a sustained transfer rate of 1.6 to 2 MB/sec as other factors come into play here.

When you're comparing product specs, ensure that you take a close look at the actual *facts* the manufacturer is talking about.

- **Burst Speed/Peak:** These numbers indicate an ›ideal‹ value i. e. the best performance the disk or controller can deliver under perfect operating conditions. This does *not* mean your studio.
- **Sustained Throughput/Low Peak:** The lowest guaranteed value, i. e. the performance of the component under the worst possible conditions—such as the actual use of LAM.

These two values will differ dramatically, so don't get suckered by the specs.

The *sustained throughput* value will tell you how many audio tracks your setup will play back reliably before you run into problems, so focus on this figure!

Speed

- Minimum data throughput specifications. Using the info above, you can estimate how many audio tracks the disk—in conjunction with the peripheral interface and the rest of your Macintosh—can play back.
- Avoid drives that ›feature‹ thermal calibration, otherwise you can look forward to years of audio ›glitches‹.
- ›Av‹ disks are highly recommended as they're designed for audio/video (A/V) applications and have a wide, continuous data stream.

Size

For most projects, 300 to 500 megabyte per song should do the trick.

An audio hard disk with at least two to three gigabytes is needed for working on four or five songs without a lot of screwing around. Get a six gigabyte or larger disk if you're planning to work with dozens of tracks, lengthy songs (remixers take note!) or compiling an album. The reasons why you need disks this big are that you *will*

- do multiple takes—›keep singing, I'll compile the best bits later‹—heard this?
- use some of this space as a ›scratchpad‹ etc. (for compiling those ›best bits‹),
- screw up, sooner or later.

Two gigabytes is a *very* tight fit for four to five songs in this context.

As general rules: the higher the storage capacity of disks, the faster the throughput. Additionally, smaller hard disks are fragmented much more quickly, which means that disk performance is degraded faster than larger capacity drives and you'll be forced to ›defrag‹ more often.

Mainboard—a. k. a. the ›Logic‹ board

This is any computer's backbone, all other component cards reside on it. I'm not going to bore you with ›what's so great about the‹ raves on the … ›Tsunami‹ board, what the difference is between the ›Nitro‹ and ›TNT‹ or why you should avoid the ›Tanzania.‹

Even if I did indulge, it wouldn't do you much good anyway—Apple rarely mentions its mainboard names in their product flyers. Instead, we'll take a quick look at the key questions you should ask about the mainboard when you're buying a computer:

- Is the CPU on a plug-in card/ZIF socket or is it hardwired? Only the plug-in/ZIF versions let you upgrade your box with a better processor later on without a ridiculous amount of hassle.

- How fast is the bus speed and will it cope with processor upgrades?
- How many RAM slots are available? Figure out what this translates to in terms of maximum RAM upgrade and ask yourself if this figure will meet future requirements.
- Are there enough PCI slots on board?
- What type of peripheral interfaces (SCSI/E-IDE/Firewire/ USB) are included and how many of these are there?

Be sure to take a long, hard look at these shopping criteria—in contrast to other computer component upgrades, swapping the entire mainboard usually doesn't pay.

The Monitor

... is your interface into the joys of Logic Audio.

My suggestion as a good—read minimum— resolution to run LAM is 1,024 × 768 pixels. Lower than this and the software is a pain in the butt to use.

With LAM's ability to instantly have multiple editing windows open with the ›Screenset‹ function, it can use up huge amounts of screen real estate. As a recommendation, go for a 17-inch screen or larger. Logic Audio also has the ability to run on multiple monitors on certain Macintoshs.

Ensure that your monitor is crisp and readable when running in the resolution that you prefer and refuse to settle for any monitor that doesn't have a refresh frequency of at least 75 Hz.

Another thing to look out for is a low-radiation monitor which has the advantage of not bombarding your recording equipment with loads of electromagnetic interference, which equals less hiss, hum and other peripheral noise in your audio signals.

To take the ›low radiation‹ vibe further ... the new LCD flat panel monitors have *no* radiation. They also look damned cool, take up very little of your desktop space and use less power than CRT monitors. The bummer is that they are expensive and their sometimes slower screen redraws. There are some LC displays which are every bit as fast as CRT monitors but expect to mortgage the house for one of these.

Back in the real world of poverty-stricken musicians ...

Any Windows PC ›multisync‹ monitor can be used for the Macintosh. If the Monitors and Sound control panel doesn't show all of the resolutions that a given monitor is able to produce, then the problem is generally due to the monitor cable or adapter. Apple has the solution—the universal Macintosh adapter. Third-party vendors also offer universal adapters that feature integrated mini-switches for adapting your setup to the monitor.

Blue and white G3s and Wallstreet Powerbooks feature a Standard SVGA port instead of the proprietary Apple monitor connector.

If you aren't planning on using your computer for professional-quality graphics and layout applications, you can make do with a compromise in true color and screen symmetry to keep a lid on your expenses.

Graphics Cards

Every Macintosh ships with at least one internal graphics card. If you want to boost the performance of your computer, a higher-quality card will sometimes do the trick.

Although the enhanced color depth that this type of card delivers isn't a big deal for LAM operation, there are two possible improvements that may benefit LAM users:

- Picture quality doesn't depend solely on the monitor; the graphics card also has a major impact. If you own a hi-res monitor and a lo-res graphics card, a higher-quality graphics card could conceivably give you both a better resolution and refresh rate.
- A quality graphics card will speed up screen redraws which is essential given LAM's screenset function and the graphic nature of the Mac Os.

In some computers (e.g. 7000 and 8000 series Power Macintoshs), you have the option of boosting the internal graphics card's performance by expanding the video RAM (4 MB of graphics memory is the minimum you should consider).

The new blue and white G3s come factory-fitted with a 16 MB ATI Rage 128 graphics card which absolutely screams.

► Emagic recommend that all blue G3 owners upgrade the video driver for their ATI card as there are some redraw issues with the driver that ships with Mac Os 8.5.1. For users running Mac Os 8.6 or higher, this driver update is included, but it's always worthwhile checking regularly for updates. More info at `http://www.apple.com/`

Backup

Removables

As hard disk recording at CD-quality (44.1 kHz) takes up 10 MB per Stereo minute (5 MB a minute in Mono), you *will* fill your hard disk(s) very, very quickly. Among the backup options are the Removable Drives, such as the Jaz (1 or 2 gigabyte), Orb (2.2 gigabyte) and the smaller Shark (250 MB) and ZIP (100 and 250 MB) drives.

The advantage of these mechanisms is that cartridges are relatively cheap to buy and they give you quick access to your data. In the case of the Jaz and Orb drives, you can even playback and record directly to them although you may find that they start to struggle if you try to play back more than eight to ten audio streams simultaneously. (Some people have actually coaxed sixteen tracks out of these mechanisms on fast machines/SCSI controllers.) The smaller capacity drives (ZIP, Shark) mentioned above are not that useful as a backup medium with large amounts of audio data (particularly 24-bit files) and neither is fast enough for direct playback of more than a few tracks, so you'll need to transfer your data to a ›working‹ drive.

CD

Another alternative is a CD Recorder—either a WORM (Write Once Read Many) or CDE (Compact Disc Erasable—a. k. a. CD-RW or ›Rewritable‹) drive. The advantages with these are:

- Blank CDs are *cheap!!!!*—and the medium, once recorded, is much less susceptible to damage over time, unlike the magnetic cartridges used by the Removable Drives. Current estimate is that your CDs should last for about 70 years.
- You can ›roll your own‹ audio CDs, that will play on any compact disc player and also keep data copies of all of your work.
- CDE Drives allow you to record and erase your data over and over to the same ›blank,‹ much like a giant floppy disk ... the bummer is that the blanks are around four to five times as expensive as the non-erasable type of CD blanks. Although both are pretty cheap these days.

A disadvantage with either type of CD drive is that neither is fast enough to read directly within LAM, so you'll need to transfer any samples required to your ›working‹ drive before creating your next masterpiece.

DAT

A third alternative is DAT/Tape Backup, which is a cheap and moderately reliable method of backup—but it's glacier slow—a one gigabyte backup or restore will take about 90 minutes.

Mo

Yet another possibility is Mo (Magneto Optical) storage. These are high capacity devices that are in between CD and hard disk as far as speed goes. However, the 5.25-inch models aren't cheap.

DVD

Lastly is recordable DVD (Digital Versatile Disk). Basically a disk that looks like a standard CD that can store up to 16 GB, with data written to both sides of the platter. This medium is in its infancy and the DVD ›standard‹ is still being finalized. Avoid this until they sort it out.

For the record, I use CDE/CDR/removable cartridges and restore to a working drive.

The Ideal LAM Macintosh

Now that you know all about what influence the key computer components and expansions have on your setup, here's a few bottom-line tips and info on buying or updating a LAM computer. There's also a section here called ›Thanks, but no thanks!‹ which covers models that you should avoid like the plague.

Blue and White G3

OK, this is the bees knees as far as the current state-of-the-art in Macintosh computing goes. There are several models ranging up from 300 MHz clock speed.

All models *above* the 300 MHz model feature a 1 MB back-side cache which runs at half the processor's clock speed. The 300 MHz model has a 512 kB cache.

All models feature (among other things):

- Four PCI slots—one is occupied by the graphics card
- An ATI Rage 128 graphics card with 16 MB of RAM
- An internal IDE hard disk (6 or 9 GB or larger)
- Two USB ports
- Two Firewire ports
- An ADB port, so the dongle is no probem.
- 64 or 128 MB RAM as standard
- Internal 16-bit/44.1 kHz sound

The 400 MHz model also comes with an Ultra-Wide SCSI controller card installed in one of the PCI slots.

I can highly recommend the blue and white G3s—I own one myself. There are three downsides to this range, however.

- The range of MIDI options available for these machines is limited. You have the choice of installing a third-party serial/modem port which will allow you to use an existing Macintosh MIDI interface or use one of a handful of USB devices. By mid to late 1999, there should be a much healthier number of USB MIDI options.
- The machines don't ship with a floppy drive which is required for the installation of Logic Audio Silver and for many VST Plug-Ins which use the PACE copy protection scheme. You should install Pace's USB Floppy Enabler—

http://www.paceap.com/iesite/ This allows the use of their copy protection with USB floppy disks.

- There are only three PCI slots available (at most).

USB Floppy Drive solutions for the Blue G3 (and iMac)

- VST Technologies—
  http://www.vsttech.com/imac_floppy.html
- Imation ›SuperDisk‹ 120 MB drive, supports floppy disks —http://www.superdisk.com/
- Newer Technologies ›uDrive‹—
  http://www.newertech.com/products/usb/
- Teac ›FD-05PU‹—
  http://www.teac.co.jp/dspd/product/fdd/fd-05pu.htm

PCI Slot Expansion Options

In the event that the three PCI slots of the G3 (blue/white) are not enough (e.g. for a big ProTools system), a PCI expansion box can be used. They can provide up to thirteen PCI slots. Powerbooks are also supported.

Some suppliers who actively support ProTools are:

- Magma, seven-slot Desktop PCI-to-PCI Expansion System—http://www.magma.com/pci/pci7dt.htm
- Promax, PCI seven-slot expansion chassis—
  http://www.promax.com/

Original or Clone?

For several years up until late 1998, Apple licensed their technology to third-party vendors. These companies built and sold Macintosh-compatible computers—a.k.a. ›clones.‹

Clones featured the same processors as original Apple computers. The motherboards were identical or slightly modified—usually the products of a joint effort by the clone maker and Apple. The big differences between the originals and forgeries are factors such as the design of the housing and number of expansion slots.

- The leading makers and resellers of Macintosh-compatible computers were Daystar, Motorola, Power Computing, Powertools, and Umax.
- There's nothing to be said against investing in a second-hand Macintosh clone as many feature better expansion options, e.g. more PCI slots. Before you fork over any dough for a Macintosh clone, however, find out exactly how long the manufacturer will continue to service the device—or indeed if they are still in business.

Rejuvenating Old Macintoshs

It wasn't too long ago that even opening a Macintosh housing was considered a cardinal sin in the Macintosh world. Nowadays, with the new blue and white G3s it's so easy your dog could do it.

When considering a hardware upgrade, focus on the two key factors in computing performance—the clock speed and CPU type:

Clock

Many upgrade kits are designed to boost the CPU frequency by replacing the crystal-controlled oscillator or similar adventurous measures. This alone won't beef up performance by a considerable margin. The upper limit of a given clock enhancement also varies from computer to computer.

CPU

The plug-in CPU card is replaced in its entirety with a current processor card. This is standard procedure for increasing the CPU frequency and delivers a much greater boost in performance.

Method 1 is best left to ambitious computer DIY nuts—I wouldn't recommend this type of home electronics experimentation. Method 2 is the way to go if your computer is ready for this kind of upgrade. For those experiencing budgetary woes, a second-hand PCI Macintosh with a slot for a processor card might get the ball rolling until your horse finally finishes first.

► When you're contemplating the upgrading of your box, bear in mind that you may be forced to also replace the Level 2 Cache to cater to the new and improved clock rate.

Thanks, But No Thanks!

Unfortunately, there are a bunch of computers that you should avoid buying for diverse reasons:

Nubus Macintoshs

Buy these types of computer only if you're absolutely convinced that you'll never need a current audio card for LAM and the computer is a steal.

Hard-wired CPU

You can't boost processor performance by plugging in a new CPU with these types of Macintoshs, i.e. the PowerMacintosh 7200, 8200 and 4400 (see below) and most PPC Performas.

PM 4400 (a.k.a. PM 7220)

The Power Macintosh 4400, as well as the many clones based on the same board design (Tanzania), are lemons. Aside from the soldered CPU, these boxes have other serious problems: There are wild deviations in the quality of components (e.g. RAM and DMA chips) which means that while one PM 4400 may work with LAM, another won't. If a smiling person offers you one, run.

The iMac

The iMac boldly goes where no computer has gone before.

- It doesn't feature a floppy disk drive which is a problem for many plug-in installations and for the installation of Logic Audio Silver (see page 43 for solutions).
- Its only expansion option is via the universal but sadly slow Universal Serial Bus (USB)—so forget about connecting another hard disk.
- Another blow is that the iMac has *no* PCI slots, so audio is limited to the internal sound capabilities. If you're not too picky with sound quality, this may be OK for you, but I wouldn't be considering any mastering on it.
- Worst of all, it doesn't have an ADB port, so Logic Audio Gold and Platinum are not an option unless you install the iMate, a USB to ADB converter from Griffin Technology `http://www.griffintechnology.com/imac/iport_driver.html`

Still, if you already own an iMac, are considering one or are on a tight budget then they may fit the bill. The internal sound hardware will deliver reasonable results (certainly better than most four to eight track tape machines) and they are fast enough to handle 24 tracks of audio and a bunch of EQs and Send Fx.

If you have a higher vision and a hankerin' for something a little more ›pro‹ with your finished results, then take a look at other computer options for LAM, but don't discount the iMac as a handy demo/pre-production machine.

What's the Deal with Powerbooks?

For many of us, a fully-equipped computer studio that can be carried around without risking permanent spinal damage is a pretty tempting concept. So what's the deal, is it possible to run LAM on a Powerbook and use it effectively as a port-a-studio?

Well yes, and no …

As general rules with Powerbooks, the shortcomings are:

- Components are designed to consume as little power as possible, and the integrated hard disks are often much slower than an equivalent desktop model, which instantly reduces the potential number of tracks.
- Their mainboards usually run on a lower voltage, which may also lead to audio processing problems.
- They don't feature standard PCI slots so you can't install the type of audio card that you may want and need for LAM.

There are PCI expansion options available (see page 44), although this reduces the ›portable‹ aspect of port-a-studio quite a bit.

On the Plus Side

All Powerbooks released over the past couple of years feature a 16-bit sound system on board, which means that you can use LAM in AV mode. To be honest, the audio quality ain't that great.

Basic tasks like arrangement, cutting and audio editing etc. can be done on a Powerbook which is useful for making a ›rough sketch‹ of a spur-of-the-moment idea.

The new G3s (a.k.a. Lombard or 101) are capable of speeds up to 400 MHz and have a 512 or 1 MB backside cache.

The main memory bus in these new machines runs at a clock speed of 66 MHz. The internal PCI bus runs at 33 MHz. To enhance performance, the Grackle IC supports concurrent transactions on the main memory bus and the PCI bus.

Audio Hardware for Powerbooks

There are a couple of serious hardware options now available in the form of PC Cards from Digigram—namely the PCX Pocket and VX Pocket hardware. Check for detailed info `http://www.digigram.com/`

To Be Considered

If you're planning on buying a Powerbook as a portable demo studio or a handy post-editing tool, some advice before you reach for your credit card:

- Go for a model with 250 MHz clock or higher.
- The Wallstreet/233 models have no level 2 cache, which LAM needs for fast audio processing. The higher-level models are OK.
- Upgrading Powerbook processors is out of the question in all but the most recent machines.
- Check the number of ADB/modem/USB ports. Some models do not have an ADB port, so forget 'em for the dongle.
- Hire or borrow the unit first to check its LAM performance otherwise you may end up with a machine that only plays back three or four audio tracks.

Lombard or 101 Powerbooks

The current G3 Powerbooks—the Lombard (101) PowerMacs—are very impressive and could definitely be used as a portable LAM studio. The only limitation being the quality of audio recording, which as mentioned, can be augmented with additional PC card hardware which delivers great results.

Another factor to consider is that these latest G3s don't have an ADB port, so Logic Audio Gold and Platinum are not an option unless you install an adapter (see page 47) or go for LAM Silver.

My bottom line on Powerbooks for LAM: I wouldn't personally use one, unless it was one of the latest G3s.

My Recommendation for LAM 4

- Blue and White G3—400 (or faster) MHz
- 128 MB (or more) of (100 MHz) SDRAM
- Mac Os 8.6
- A USB floppy drive
- Sound Hardware of choice—Audiowerk 8 recommended
- MIDI Hardware of choice—Unitor 8 (with Stealth port or AMT 8)/AMT 8 recommended
- More hard disk space than you could possibly use (you'll find a way)—SCSI Ultra Wide or Firewire multiple drives.
- CD-R or CD-Rw for backup

Don't play games, try out shareware or download stuff from the Internet on this machine!

How Many Tracks and Fx Will I Get?

At this point, I guess you might be wondering what you can expect from your hardware in terms of performance. Below are some stats on a few ›standard‹ computer configurations which are a rough performance guide.

Processor	RAM	Audio tracks	Fx
PPC 603e/180	128 MB	up to 32	plus up to 8 EQ and/or 2 to 4 Fx
PPC 604e/200	128 MB	32 to 64	plus up to 16 EQ and/or 2 to 8 Fx
PPC 750/300	128 MB	up to 128 (req. hardware)	plus up to 24 EQ and/or 2 to 10 Fx
B&W PPC 750/400	128 MB	up to 128 (req. hardware)	plus 24 EQ and 2 to 16 Fx

The requirements are:

- Running LAM Platinum (4).
- All machines above equipped with an Audiowerk 8 card.
- All machines with Ultra Wide SCSI controller and hard disks. On the Blue G3 with Firewire, the Fx performance could be increased as a result of less CPU activity.
- EQ: LAM-internal EQ rather than a third-party EQ plug-in.
- Plug-in: internal LAM plug-in rather than a third-party Fx plug-in. The range of Fx depends on the type of algorithm used. Reverbs can use vast amounts of processing power in comparison to flangers, EQs or compressors.
- Performance specs are estimates; in an optimally configured computer with the fastest peripherals money can buy, you may come up with way better results. Conversely, if your machine doesn't have the right components, your results may be worse.
- The estimated number of tracks figures are heavily reliant on the type and specification of hard disks, the peripheral bus used (IDE, SCSI or Firewire) and soundcards.

When looking at this table, account for the fact that LAM's internal EQs and Fx plug-ins are not exactly CPU vultures. Once you're over the ›new toy‹ thing, you'll probably want to add a third party plug-in or two, which will (generally) force the computer to work harder. In this context, you should go for the biggest, baddest monster Macintosh that you can afford, 'cos believe me, you (and your plug-ins) will quickly get to that ›need for speed‹ point where upgrading becomes necessary... and then the sad ›gear—lust‹ cycle will begin, again!

3 Sound and MIDI Hardware for Use with LAM

Ahhh—The $64,000 question.

LAM Platinum ›directly‹ supports a number of audio interfaces allowing fast, unhindered access to their functions. The Gold and Silver versions offer support for Macintosh AV and the Audiowerk2 and 8 cards.

Below is a hardware list that Platinum supports.

- Akai DR8/16 (Arrange Editing only)
- ASIO Devices
- AV Support—internal Stereo Audio I/O
- DAE—Digidesign Audio Engine (AudiomediaII, III)
- DAE—Project Driver Mode (Session8, ProTools Project)
- Digidesign Direct I/O (AMIII, Project II)
- Digidesign TDM (ProTools PTIII/24)
- Emagic Audiowerk8 (three simultaneous cards supported)
- Korg 1212 I/O
- Sonorus STUDI/O
- Yamaha CBX
- Yamaha DSP Factory (DS2416)

For devices that are not directly supported, Emagic offers ASIO support which is covered in the section entitled ASIO on page 68.

Below, soundcard terminology is explained, but first I'd like to cover a couple of neat new things in version 4.

NB: ›Direct‹ support of many devices actually involves an additional software layer, such as the DAE which LAM ›talks‹ to rather than communicating *directly* with the hardware. This software layer allows access to any additional functionality, such as DSP, that the hardware may feature. As Emagic is reliant on the hardware manufacturers to provide them with an API suitable for this support, some functionality available to the hardware may *not* be accessible in LAM.

New in Version 4

New EASI Driver Interface

EASI (Enhanced Audio Streaming Interface) is Emagic's new soundcard interface. This is somewhat similar in concept to ASIO and allows hardware manufacturers to write drivers which will work more efficiently within LAM. Technically, it's quite different to ASIO and, at the time of writing, a number of soundcard and other manufacturers have been approached. The first devices supported by EASI are Emagic's Audiowerk and the Sonorus STUDI/O. In fact the ›direct‹ driver in LAM 4.0 for these devices is an EASI driver.

Relaunch Feature

This neat feature allows you to activate new hardware within LAM without the need to reboot either the software or your Macintosh. The latter requires that any drivers/extensions needed by the audio device are already installed on the machine.

This is extremely handy for anyone running Digidesign hardware and switching between DAE and Direct I/O or ASIO modes.

► On switching the hardware, the Relaunch automatically prompts you with a dialog box. Just click ›Try (Re)Launch.‹ Just to be safe, save your current song before using this function!

Direct I/O for Digidesign Hardware

Owners of Digidesign hardware now have an improved Direct I/O option in the Audio Hardware Setup window. Check out the differences:

Direct I/O

- allows the use of LAM's internal (CPU-based) effects
- supports stereo interleaved files

- no scrubbing
- no access to any DSP hardware

DAE

- LAM's internal FX can *not* be used (except ›offline‹ i.e. non-realtime plugins in Premiere/Audiosuite format).
- no support for stereo interleaved files
- allows scrubbing of audio
- access to DSP hardware for EQ etc.

Audio Converters

All digital audio recording systems have to ›convert‹ the sound from analog information into digital information at least once so the computer can deal with it. The ›analog‹ information I'm talking about here is sound that we hear in the ›real‹ as opposed to computer world.

The conversion is achieved using an ADC (Analog to Digital Converter) when you are recording information. When you play back info (sound) it will go through a reverse process using the DAC (Digital to Analog Converter).

Most soundcard spec sheets will proudly announce that they do ›16 bit, 44.1 kHz‹ or ›CD quality‹ recording and you may be wondering why some cards cost a couple of hundred dollars and some cost thousands.

The answer lies in the quality of the ADC/DAC and other components on the card. Generally, (though not always) the more expensive the card, the better these components will be, which results in clearer and less noisy recordings.

Recently, there has been a (much hyped) change from 16-bit to 20- or 24-bit recording in the pro and semi-pro market. A lot of devices will feature specs such as: 20/24-bit ›processing.‹ What this means is that the audio is still being recorded and played back at 16 bits, but the audio files are dealt with internally at a higher resolution, resulting in (theoretically) cleaner sound, particularly when editing.

Don't get too hung up on specs though, ›true‹ 20/24-bit recording and higher sample rates like 96 kHz are not likely to supplant 16-bit, 44.1-kHz recording for some time. The reason—consumer playback devices such as DVD players are not yet widely available and a lot of people will object to yet another format when they're already happy with the quality of CD.

LAM 4, as with previous versions, features 32-bit internal audio processing. In plain-speak, this means that any editing/processing done on your samples will be more precise and the results will (potentially) be better sounding.

Digital Interfaces

Many soundcards in the mid to high-end price range feature digital interfaces which allow you to transfer audio data to and from an external device—like a DAT machine or digital mixing console—with no loss of signal quality. The main interfaces available are:

S/P-DIF I/O

Sony/**P**hilips-**D**igital **I**nter**F**ace, ›I/O‹ is short for ›**I**nput/**O**utput.‹

S/P-DIF is the most commonly found digital interface with many soundcards featuring an S/P-DIF I/O as either their *only* interface or in conjunction with an analog interface.

S/P-DIF transmits and receives in stereo and 16 bit and supports sample rates up to 48 kHz.

If you own a DAT recorder and/or digital mixer which features S/P-DIF, you should seriously consider a card that features these types of connectors.

ADAT and TDIF I/O

Both of these interfaces allow the transfer of eight digital signals (mono tracks) simultaneously using one cable in each direction (in and out) from a single pair of connectors. Obviously the transfer of eight tracks rather than S/P-DIF's stereo transfer limitation has a number of advantages.

If you own a Tascam digital recorder, you should definitely go for an interface featuring TDIF (**T**ascam **D**igital **I**nter**F**ace). If you own, or are planning to buy, equipment from other manufacturers, the ADAT multi-channel interface by Alesis is well established. This is an optical interface featuring a fiber-optic cable, which has a number of practical advantages, including use over much longer distances and greater resistance to electromagnetic interference.

If you decide on a card that features any type of digital interface, you can use the converters in your DAT, ADAT or digital mixing console and route exclusively digital signals to and from the Macintosh.

Supported Devices

A detailed guide to all Macintosh-compatible soundcards and audio systems would be about 400 pages thick, so in both our interests, I'll only discuss cards that are directly supported by LAM or have a large user base.

Many of these and other devices also feature ASIO driver support (or at least have an ASIO driver ›in the works,‹ so if *your* hardware isn't mentioned here, check the CD-ROM for an updated list). At the time of writing, it was a little early to know which manufacturers would be writing EASI drivers, but where possible, I've included these.

The first step in your quest for the perfect device for your needs, is to figure out the number of audio inputs and outputs you require now and in the foreseeable future. It would be simple if the difference between low and high-end systems was based purely on the number of I/Os, but this ain't the way it is.

Your choice should also depend on the way you work ... but all isn't lost if you shell out on something now that you quickly outgrow. You can always add extra hardware later as you can afford it and when you need it.

Stereo I/O Devices

If you use the ›overdub‹ recording method—i. e. one instrument after another—and execute all audio editing and processing tasks on your computer, then a card featuring a single stereo input and output will do just fine:

For Those on a Tight Budget—Macintosh Internal Sound (AV)

All Apple computers that are suitable for LAM ship with an on-board 16-bit sound system.

How Does a Macintosh Sound?

Apple G3 computers feature integrated audio hardware that sounds *way* better than that found in older models. If you don't want to invest in an additional audio card, and aren't too fussy, the internal audio hardware might suffice.

But ...

The Macintosh audio hardware is limited to a single stereo input and output. It lets you record audio at a ›CD standard‹ 16-bit/44.1-kHz rate and generate CD Masters ... *not!!!*

You should note that the ›CD standard‹ 16 bit/44.1 kHz refers to the technical format of the files, not their audio quality!

The Macintosh audio system is fine for demo productions, but it certainly won't replace a professional audio card.

Optimizing Audio Quality

If you want to, or are forced to, work exclusively with the Macintosh audio hardware, don't despair, here are a few ›tricks‹ that will improve the quality of your recordings:

- Although a microphone symbol often graces the stereo 1/8-inch input, never plug a microphone directly into this input unless you're a ›lo-fi junkie.‹ Invest in a decent studio microphone and a suitable preamp. Patch a line signal from the preamp to your Macintosh.
- Even if your Macintosh model is equipped with additional RCA audio inputs, use the minijack instead because it has a signal-to-noise ratio that is some 6 dB higher, which means there will be less hiss in your recording(s).
- Pre-mix signals that belong together anyway—e.g. stacked keyboard sounds—to make a single mono or stereo recording instead of recording each separately. The fewer recording operations that you can get by with, the less unwanted noise you'll end up with in your mix.
- Never record loops from audio sampling CDs via the analog ins—always import this audio data digitally via the CD-ROM drive of your computer. If at all possible, stick to special sampling CD-ROMs that let you import material directly in AIF format.

Emagic Audiowerk2—EASI and ASIO

- PCI, 2 × Analog In, 2 × Analog Out, S/P-DIF I/O, 20-bit converter, Audio RCA jacks
- Allows simultaneous use of digital and analog outs for 4-channel output. No slave sync possible. Good inexpensive card.

Digidesign Audiomedia II—DAE

- Nubus; 2 × In, 2 × Out (analog and S/P-DIF) RCA jacks

- This card is old, a little noisy and Nubus. Only suitable for 68k Macintoshs and a handful of 601-based PowerMacintoshs. Even if you own one of these older machines, you'd be hard-pressed to find an AMII and I would suggest that you spend that money elsewhere—say on buying a Macintosh with PCI slots.

Digidesign Audiomedia III—DAE and Direct I/O

- PCI; 2 × In, 2 × Out (analog and S/P-DIF), RCA jacks, internal DSP for EQ
- The card's features are impressive, and it sounds good.

Multi I/O Devices

If you occasionally want to record or playback more than just a stereo signal, like an individually-miked drum kit, a string quartet or an entire band, you should look at other hardware which features multiple inputs and outputs.

Most Multi-I/O cards presently on the market, however, are limited to a single stereo *analog* input, but feature eight or more audio outputs. When you use LAM with one of these cards, you have an enhanced master section with lots 'o individual outputs giving you much more flexibility, particularly if you use outboard FX.

► With some existing hardware such as Korg's 1212 I/O, Sonorus and ProDIF hardware which feature an optical interface, it is possible to route multiple channels of audio into/out of LAM in a single pass *digitally*. MOTU's 2408 can record through eight analog and up to sixteen digital (optical) inputs simultaneously.

Take a closer look at this type of card if you're thinking of using LAM in conjunction with an external multi-track recorder, mixing console and/or hardware effects processors.

Emagic Audiowerk 8—EASI

- PCI, 2 × Analog In, 8 × Analog Out, S/P-DIF I/O, 20-bit converter. Audio RCA jacks in a ›breakout‹ cable which is RF shielded.
- Up to three units can be used simultaneously for multiple outputs
- A great choice for use with LAM. It sounds good and gives you lots of tracks, places almost no overhead on the CPU of the host Macintosh and most importantly, is manufactured by the company who makes the software, so there are no conflicts.

Echo Event DARLA—ASIO

At the time of writing, the ASIO drivers for the Event hardware were problematic on the ›blue‹ G3s. Check our support page (see page 181) for the latest info in this regard *before* you spend your hard-earned. For beige G3 and other PowerMacintosh owners, this should not be a problem.

- PCI, 2 × Analog In, 8 × Analog Out, 20-bit converter. Audio RCA jacks in an Adapter Box that is mounted directly to the metal slot frame.
- DARLA is inexpensive and like all of the Event cards—according to independent bench tests—has very good

audio specifications. If you don't anticipate the need for a digital interface, then DARLA is recommended.

Echo Event GINA—ASIO

- PCI, features identical to DARLA (2 × Analog In, 8 × Analog Out, 20-bit converter), although with additional S/P-DIF I/O, which can be used in LAM (i. e. a max. of 4 × In, 10 × Out). Also an external box equipped with analog audio interfaces in the form of phone jacks.

Echo Event LAYLA—ASIO

- PCI, 8 × Analog In, 10 × Analog Out, 20-bit converter, S/P-DIF I/O, Wordclock I/O, MIDI-In/Out/Thru, cascadable. Ports housed in an external 19-inch box.
- Currently the most professional of the Event devices

Korg 1212 I/O—ASIO

- PCI, 2 × Analog I/O (20-bit A/D, 18-bit D/A converter), S/P-DIF I/O, 8-channel ADAT I/O, ADAT Sync-In, Wordclock Sync
- In LAM, you can use all inputs and outputs simultaneously (a max. of twelve-way I/O).
- With only two-way analog I/O but ten-way digital I/O, I can only recommend this card to users of ADAT or ADAT-compatible devices such as digital mixers. However, because of its price, the card is a good buy for this type of application.

Sonorus STUDI/O—EASI

- PCI, Analog Stereo Out, 2 × Optical I/O, you can use each of them either as S/P-DIF- or 8-Channel ADAT I/O. In LAM, you can use a maximum of 16 Ins and 18 Outs simultaneously. The concept is much like a ›double‹ Korg 1212 I/

O, although you should be aware that it isn't equipped with an analog input.

PRODIF Platinum—ASIO

- Features are identical to those of the Sonorus STUDI/O.

Mark of the Unicorn 2408—ASIO

- PCI, external 19-inch box with 8 × Analog In (RCA), 2 × Analog Out, 20-bit converters; 3 × ADAT, 3 × TDIF interface, 1 × S/P-DIF In, 2 × S/P-DIF Out and RS 422 interface for synchronization.
- A total of seven 8-channel banks (3 × Tascam and 3 × ADAT as well as 1 × analog) can be assigned internally to three 8-channel I/O busses, which enables you to access a maximum of 24 simultaneous inputs or outputs, depending on the recording situation.
- The jury is out with regards to its audio quality. Many users feel it is great while others are unconvinced. Use your own ears to decide.
- The MotU system's versatile concept is impressive, as is its price. It retails for somewhere in the range of $ 1,000, which is unheard of for a system that delivers this level of options.

Multi I/O Devices with DSP Functionality

Increasingly, inexpensive Macintosh sound hardware featuring internal DSP computing power is hitting the market. What this means to you is that additional filters, compressors or multi-effects are actually computed by the card, taking the strain off the CPU. In other words, you can enjoy the use of as many LAM EQS and/or plug-ins as you would normally have *plus* the additional DSP performance of the soundcard!

Up until recently, however, systems with dedicated DSP were exclusively the domain of the rich and famous. Some still are. Examples of systems at the upper end of the scale include: Ensoniq Paris, Digidesign's ProTools and Creamware's Scope.

Digidesign ProTools 24/24 MIX/MIX PLUS—TDM

I have only included this latest of Digidesign systems as it makes previous systems somewhat obsolete. See the sidebar.

Digidesign have, as usual, been trying to get everyone to upgrade to the new MIX systems. Compared to the Pro Tools 24 system, MIX PLUS will give you 32 tracks with dynamics and EQ on every track, five sends on every track, about ten or so delay FX and a couple of TC Works Mega-reverbs. The PT24 system will only give one reverb, 24 tracks and a couple of sends with no EQ or dynamics processing.

- PCI, variable number of Analog Ins and Analog Outs via various 19-inch rackmount expansion options, S/P-DIF I/O, optional ADAT I/O, 24 bit/96 kHz.
- Great sounding, stable and expensive system.
- Requires a *lot* of RAM. Start at 192 MB.
- Dedicated EQ and dynamics processing hardware on Mix Core system (based around d24 card).
- Has additional dedicated DSP hardware on separate ›farm‹ card (6 × Motorola 56301).
- The MIX PLUS system has both a Core and Farm card.
- Multiple cards can be used for additional DSP and the load between mixing and FX processing is shared between available resources.
- Each card supports up to sixteen additional I/O.
- MIX Farm cards can be added to existing PT24 systems.
- See `digicompat` PDF document on CD-ROM for more detail.

At the ›budget‹ end of the scale, two cards with some fairly heavy-duty DSP grunt which have created quite a stir are the …

Yamaha DSP Factory—Direct and ASIO

- Basic PCI card DS2416 with 2 × Analog I/O (20-bit converter) each and S/P-DIF I/O.

- Among other features, the DSP capacity comprises an internal digital mixer similar to the Yamaha 02R/03D with ten Bus Outs, six Aux Sends, parametric 4-Band EQs with a total of 104 frequency bands, 26 dynamic processors for compressors/gates, etc. as well as two REV500 multi-effects processors.
- The system manages up to eight input and sixteen output signals internally. With appropriate expansions, you can access these circuits via physical audio interfaces. The Ax44 expansion for example offers 4 × Analog I/O each and a Headphones Out.
- Additional expansions featuring digital interfaces are in the works. Both the basic card and the interface expansions are cascadable, so you can upgrade the system to a maximum of 16 inputs and 32 outputs.
- When using the Yamaha card, you can use LAM's or VST Fx as inserts, but as soon as the audio is passed thru the DSP2416's onboard mixing DSPs it can *not* be further affected by anything other than its internal FX.

Creamware Pulsar/Pulsar Plus—ASIO

While it's a little early to be talking about the Pulsar on the Macintosh as its control software development is well behind that of the Windows version, I thought I'd include it here for future reference.

- PCI, 20-bit ADC, 24-bit DAC, 2 × Analog I/O, ADAT optical I/O and S/P-DIF I/O
- Plus version also features 2 × AES/EBU I/O
- Supports sampling rates up to 96 kHz
- Worth mentioning are the external Creamware Converter Units A8 (1 × ADAT I/O ⇔ 8-Channel Analog I/O) and A16 (2 × ADAT I/O ⇔ 16-Channel Analog I/O), which can also be used with other ADAT I/O-based soundcards.

- Pulsar features four Sharc DSPs which can be used for internal audio mixing, sample playback, adding FX and synthesis.
- Despite all of this DSP power, if you wanna run LAM with Pulsar, you require a very grunty computer with *lots* of RAM. Go directly to 128 MB.
- Conceptually, this card (and its big brother Scope) is incredible as it truly represents the concept of a studio in a box, where the computer controls all of the DSP functions of the card. This allows you to create and play synth sounds using a variety of synthesis methods, play back samples in real time as you would with a sampling keyboard, record and playback hard disk audio, add dynamics processing, EQ and other FX and mix all of these together to create a final master.
- If you have the money, you can expand Pulsar using the SRB (Sonic Rocket Booster) or by using it in conjunction with the Scope system. The SRB is an add-on card that adds four SHARC DSPs to the existing four on the Pulsar card. This effectively doubles the processing power which can be used in any way you choose—for mixing, synthesis, FX etc. Up to three cards (SRB or Pulsar) can be linked via the Pulsar's proprietary internal S/TDM bus which is much faster than the PCI bus thereby avoiding latency between the cards.
- Potentially, Pulsar will be a great card for use with LAM and if the level of integration allows direct routing within LAM itself, this will be one of *the* most flexible music-making options available.

Although not immediately apparent, many of the other soundcards also feature onboard DSPs. The cards by Echo/Event, for instance, all come with an integrated 24-bit Motorola DSP (56301). According to Event, the company is ›hard at work creating drivers that will unleash the potential of the currently dormant DSPs to provide users with additional effects resources.‹

Watch this space to see what happens …

External Units with Limited Support

Two curiosities which are ›kind of‹ supported by LAM are …

Yamaha CBX-D5/D3—Direct

- External boxes connected via SCSI
- The CBX-D3 gives four outputs and two inputs.
- The D5 adds an SPX-100 signal processor and four channels of four-band parametric equalization.
- These units are *old* and obsolete.
- Two units can be chained together but if they are both CBX-D5s only the first unit's DSP can be used.
- Bottom line … look elsewhere.

Akai DR8/16—Direct

- External boxes connected via SCSI, Analog: 8 In/16 Out plus stereo master (8 In/8 Out on DR8), switchable +4/–10dB line levels; balanced 1/4-inch TSR In/Out; built-in mic preamps
- Digital: AES/EBU and S/P DIF standard
- Optional ADAT multi-channel interface
- Wordclock input standard
- Optional SMPTE, MIDI, RS 422 (Sony 9-pin), and biphase sync boards
- Optional 8- or 16-channel digital 3-band parametric EQ
- Multiple units can be chained together for more tracks.

- In LAM you can *only* do Arrange window editing with these units. This means that you have no access to the CPU-based FX or sample editing functions of LAM.

All about Drivers

Direct Support

Direct hardware support within LAM is the ideal solution. Since the driver is integrated within LAM, it does what it is supposed to without any hassles. The downside: Direct support doesn't help you if you don't own one of the devices mentioned above.

EASI

Emagic's own ›standard‹ for manufacturers of sound hardware. It consists of a programming interface that allows LAM to communicate directly with the card. This means reduced latency, fewer (or no) glitches in performance and more tracks and FX. Time will tell how well this new method of sound/software integration is accepted and adopted by various companies.

ASIO

ASIO drivers are usually optimized for use with Steinberg's Cubase VST, so it is very likely that use of an EASI driver—if available for your sound hardware—will work much more efficiently.

In essence, an ASIO driver is a modular software interface via which audio data is transported

- to LAM from the sound system (recording) and
- from LAM to the sound system (playback)

The advantage of ASIO drivers is that it opens up a whole range of serious hardware options, so you can freely pick the sound hardware that appeals most to your sensibilities and/or budget—provided it has an ASIO driver.

- reduced or (almost) no latency

- lower CPU overheads
- potentially more tracks
- potentially more Fx
- potential of access to any special DSP functions that the card may offer
- potential of access to multiple I/O functionality if available

The Apple Sound Manager

The integrated 16-bit audio hardware of a Macintosh requires a standardized software interface to allow programs such as LAM to input and output audio. In the MacOS, this is the Sound Manager system extension.

Instead of the rather spartan ›Monitors and sound‹ control panel options, LAM features its own dialog boxes where you can define the input and output parameters/driver delays etc.

Sound Manager as an Audio Middleman

If LAM can't actually communicate with a particular piece of audio hardware and there is no appropriate EASI or ASIO driver available, you do have an option, albeit a limited one: Most Macintosh-compatible audio cards let you interface them directly to the Sound Manager. What happens here is that the internal Macintosh sound system is disabled and the audio card's stereo input and outputs are used instead.

In a round-about manner, you can interface stereo I/O audio cards to LAM via the Sound Manager. However, there are a bunch of disadvantages to this type of setup and it should only be considered a temporary solution at best.

Here's how:

You will need a software driver for the audio card to link it to the Apple Sound Manager; it should have been included in the factory package with your sound hardware.

1 Copy this hardware-specific driver to the Extensions folder in the Macintosh System folder.

2 Unfortunately, you can't select the new audio hardware directly in the control field Monitors and Sound. You first have to install the Sound control panel, which you'll find on your Mac Os System CD or on Apple's Internet support pages, so if you haven't installed it—do it!

3 After you've installed the control panel, you can activate the alternative audio hardware. Depending on the hardware that you're dealing with (and more importantly its Sound Manager driver), you may have other options available.

4 Now the audio hardware should be active in the Sound Manager. Check if the system's sounds are automatically routed through this hardware.

5 If the audio card interfaces properly with the Sound Manager, you can talk to it via the Av device flip menu in your Audio Driver preferences in LAM.

6 You should now be able to address a stereo input and output of the audio card via Av audio objects in LAM.

This type of DIY interface to audio hardware via the Sound Manager has the following disadvantages:

- Setup is limited to one stereo input and output, 16-bit quality at the max, regardless of the hardware
- It increases the CPU load on your computer which equals problems such as latency and sluggish system response.

So, in summation:

If LAM directly supports your soundcard, go for it. It doesn't get any better than this.

If direct support is unavailable for your sound hardware, you need an EASI, ASIO or, in the worst case, Sound Manager driver.

Otherwise you won't be able to record/playback audio signals into/from LAM, which would be pointless really ...

What Sort of MIDI Interface Should I Use with LAM?

This is not a rundown on the relative merits of specific interfaces (although I will recommend a couple later on), but rather some good advice on selection of an appropriate interface for your needs. Additionally, there's a special section for owners (or potential owners) of the new ›blue‹ G3 PowerMacintoshs which covers USB.

The questions you should ask yourself are:

- How many ports do I need to cater to all of my MIDI devices?
- How many ports *will* I need in the foreseeable future?
- Will I need multiple input channels simultaneously?

As a general observation of MIDI musicians, you will always add new gear to your MIDI rig, you'll buy/sell/update as the years go by and you'll end up with racks full of boxes with blinking lights and at least two keyboards. While this is not true of *every*one, it is certainly true of most of us with this ›condition‹ which ends up with you becoming a blithering MIDIot—so I guess what I'm saying here is ›look to the future.‹

Synchronization ... Do I Need It?

Many MIDI interfaces also allow SMPTE/MTC and other forms of synchronization which allows you to stripe/read timecode off tape/video/hard disk and other MIDI devices that send sync information. If you work with tape (analog or digital) or video/post etc., then SMPTE is an essential component—potential advertising jingle writers or film/video soundtrack guys and girls take note!

If your needs are more modest, and all you're really going to be doing is MIDI based and recording all of your audio to the hard disk and mastering straight to DAT or CD, then sync may not be needed. Look at your current working methods or future work that may come your way and work it out.

Macintosh MIDI Drivers/OMS

LAM has its own built-in MIDI driver that is aware of a number of MIDI devices, such as the Unitor8/AMT8, simple one in/out interfaces and MOTU's MIDI Time Piece (that's what the MTP Mode is for—other interfaces will also work in MTP ›emulation‹ mode with this checkbox enabled). It also has options which allow the use of the Apple MIDI Manager and/or OMS for unrecognized devices.

Apple MIDI Manager

Despite LAM's built-in drivers, many MIDI devices installed on your system must be accompanied by a MIDI Manager compatible software driver (system extension) which does two things.

- Firstly, it lets the Mac OS ›know‹ about the hardware and what it does.
- Secondly it allows MIDI aware applications (like LAM) running on Mac OS access to the hardware's features.

About OMS

Another method of getting the Macintosh to ›see‹ the MIDI interface is via the ›standard‹ API used by many manufacturers for writing Macintosh MIDI drivers called OMS (Open MIDI System).

Essentially what happens when OMS is installed on your Macintosh—along with any MIDI drivers that ship with your interface—a global OMS extension is added to your System folder. Also installed is an OMS control panel applet.

This applet interrogates the Macintosh's serial and modem ports looking for MIDI interfaces and then takes it a step further by looking for devices connected to any interfaces that it finds.

LAM, in turn, talks to OMS rather than the MIDI port (or more accurately, its driver) directly.

The downside is that unless there's an OMS driver written specifically for the MIDI interface, then OMS (and LAM, in turn) won't see it.

Up until recently, OMS and LAM were temperamental bedfellows at best, so if you own (or are considering buying) an interface that requires OMS, make sure that you:

- download the latest version of OMS,
- are running the latest version of LAM,
- have the latest version of the OMS driver for the device,
- check its performance doing *everything* you can do with the interface (syncing, multiport record/play etc.).

Whichever way you go ... the single most important factor for your MIDI hardware is its software. If the software is badly written then no amount of ›tweaking‹ to your system will make it work the way you expect it to.

Blue and White G3 MIDI Options

This new generation of Macintoshs has forgone the modem and printer ports of previous models in favor of USB (Universal Serial Bus).

USB has the following advantages over the old serial ports:

- It is ›hot-swappable,‹ which means that you can plug/unplug the interface while the computer is running.
- The bus speed is *much* faster than the old serial ports and much faster than MIDI requires, so data throughput is not ever going to be a problem.

- You can ›daisy-chain‹ (or run off a USB ›hub‹) as many interfaces as you need. USB supports up to 127 devices!
- You can use your interface(s) on new Mac OS and Windows PCs.

The disadvantage of USB-only Macintoshs is that:

- The number of USB MIDI interfaces available is limited (although this may have changed by the time you read this).
- Existing (and perhaps expensive) MIDI interfaces that you may have been using on your ›old‹ Macintosh won't work without a serial port adapter, like those listed below. Obviously, these don't come free!

Serial Port Adapter solutions for the Blue G3

NB: Simple USB to Serial Converter plugs don't work. These converters cannot handle the external clock rate which is required by MIDI interfaces.

- **gPort**—`http://www.griffintechnology.com/g3/gport.html`
- **Stealth Serial Port**—`http://www.geethree.com/`

These two cards for the G3 provide a familiar modem port for external connections. They fit in the internal modem port instead of using a PCI slot.

- **Remus/2 or Romulus/4** PCI cards—
  `http://www.megawolf.com/`

These cards provide two or four serial interfaces on a PCI card (also for beige G3s) but MIDI interfaces only function at single speed (1 MHz), which means Fast-Mode is not possible with these cards.

About AMT

Emagic have devised a technology called AMT (Active MIDI Transmission) which relies on a combination of MIDI hardware and software to work its miracles.

This magic essentially allows the equivalent of parallel transmission of MIDI data (which is a serial protocol—i.e.

one event after the other—in ›series‹) through a sophisticated buffering system. What this means to you is that MIDI timing is absolutely accurate with multichannel events that occur on the same bar/beat/clock tick arriving at your various MIDI devices simultaneously. Presently, the only hardware devices to support this are the Unitor8 and the USB-based AMT8.

At the time of writing, Steinberg had agreed to integrate the AMT technology into future products and Emagic were involved in discussions with a number of other MIDI software and hardware vendors.

Bottom line—if you have a lot of MIDI devices and the money to afford multiple Unitor8/AMT8 units, go for it.

About AMT2

Emagic have recently updated AMT to version 2 which improves the MIDI thru handling. For anyone who owns a Unitor8 with version 1.29 firmware, you can upgrade to AMT 2 by installing version 1.06 of the Unitor8 control panel software. Contained in this installer is MIDI file data which can be sent to the Unitor8. Check the documentation for further details on the procedure (on the CD-ROM in the Emagic Folder).

Conclusions and Recommendations

Great multiport choices include the MOTU MIDI Express Macintosh and MTPII. (which I have personally used for years) and I can also strongly recommend the Unitor8/AMT8 units. AMT really *does* make a difference to the timing.

For simpler setups with only a single in/out or a few ports, I can recommend the MIDIman range. They make no frills, no fuss devices that get the job done and don't cost the earth.

I can't say I'm a fan of OMS running in conjunction with LAM as it's been the cause of much grief over the years for many users, particularly in the areas of MIDI timing and synchronization. To be fair though, the overwhelming majority of these problems seem to have been ironed out with the most recent releases of OMS and drivers from a number of manufacturers. Hopefully, this new level of stability will continue.

Opcode make great interfaces, many of which work in MTP emulation mode under LAM, so definitely give them a look. They also work with OMS drivers, so should you wish to use OMS with these interfaces, follow the tips mentioned in the OMS section on page 72.

4 Setting Up

Just before we get into the down and dirty aspects of using LAM, I'd like to cover some basic ›housekeeping‹ tasks to avoid problems later.

Up and Running

If you're using EASI, ASIO or directly supported hardware with LAM, you may need to set this up in the Audio Extensions Window (Audio Menu > Audio Hardware and Drivers).

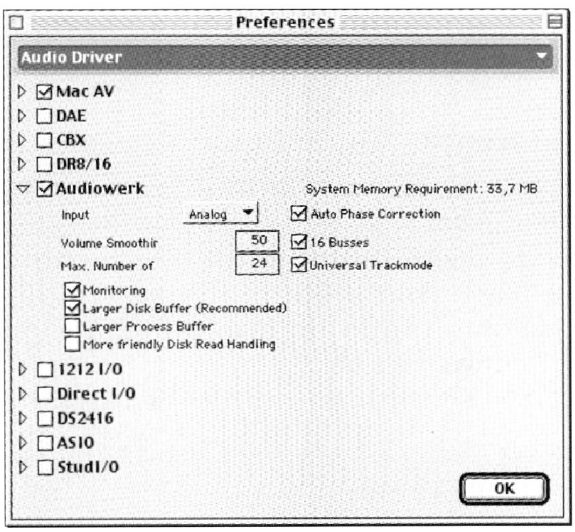

Audio Hardware Selection Panel

Simply click in the appropriate check box for your hardware. You may be prompted to ›Restart‹ by LAM to make your new hardware active.

Audio Environment Setup

LAM 4 will interrogate your hardware when using the audio hardware page and will automatically set up a default environment appropriate to the facilities of the card.

What this means, in simpler terms, is that LAM will only set up *one* master fader object if your card (and its driver) is a stereo out only device. For devices with multiple outputs, LAM will assign and automatically cable the appropriate number of objects.

Should you wish to save these settings in another song, simply open both the new and existing songs and use the Import Layer option in the Environment window of the song you wish to copy the audio objects to.

► Periodically, you may receive an ›Error Syncing Audio/MIDI‹ message. In this scenario, you can fix the problem in many cases by using the Calibrate to Internal Hardware function found in the Options menu of the Audio window.

All about Latency

›Latency‹—in a digital recording system—is the time it takes for the audio signal to be routed from the audio input to the output. As *all* digital audio systems require an amount of processing time to do this, latency is found in all digital hardware and software—including hardware digital reverbs and mixers and software effects.

The equation for a sampling rate of 44.1 kHz:

- number of samples × (1,000 ms/44,100 samples) = latency in milliseconds

Example:

- Latency = 1,056 Samples × (1,000 ms/44,100 samples) = approx. 24 ms

At this latency value, when you're monitoring an audio recording, you'll hear the signal 24 ms later than the audio at the input—i. e. what you're playing or singing will lag behind when it comes through your speakers. With this level of latency, your playing will probably start to suck as your brain tries to reconcile the timing differences. Most people find 10 to 12 ms tolerable, but this is a *very* personal thing.

So, How Do You Minimize the Effects of Latency?

First off, a faster computer and a better audio card with a direct driver will often improve things, but I know that as a musician, scraping together the cash ain't that easy. Before you reach for the razor-blades … there is a workaround for you folks with an unsupported soundcard if the system doesn't deliver the results you were expecting:

1. Simply record a MIDI track (use staccato notes—no pads—mid to high octaves),
2. Then record the output of your sound module to an audio track.
3. Listen to them both.

You'll probably find that they're a bit ›out‹ and this delay between the MIDI and audio tracks is equal to your system's latency.

To fix it, you can certainly use tricks like track delays (which can be positive or negative values) in your playback parameters for audio and/or MIDI tracks, but this will have to be done on every track for nearly every song you record for all eternity. If your idea of a good night out involves dungeons, branding-irons and humiliation, this may be for you, but most people will get over it pretty quickly.

Here's the solution:

1. Set a cycle and start playback by pressing play on the transport bar or keypad.
2. Open the Audio Menu > Audio Hardware and Drivers window.

3 When you open the flip menu for your hardware, you'll find a Driver Delay checkbox. Simply use your mouse in the value window and click/scroll up or down to adjust the value until you hear the MIDI/ audio in sync.

Et voilà!

Setting a Recording Level

For most devices, LAM has no direct facility for setting a recording level internally. You will need to use your sound hardware's own mixer applet (if available), or an external mixing console to set your levels correctly.

For some devices, you can alter the Input Gain via the flip menu options for your hardware in the Audio Hardware and Drivers window.

Digital audio, unlike analog, has no room for error. If you exceed the threshold of 0 dB DFS (Digital Full Scale), you will introduce digital artifacts such as aliasing or clipping into your recordings and believe me, you don't want this unless your music has a distinctly Nine Inch Nails flavor.

► It is always worthwhile listening to at least 30 to 60 seconds of your program material (incoming audio) to ensure that no peaks exceed the threshold.

Once your levels are set, start recording.

About Digital Audio Transfers and Word Clock

Transferring digital audio data in LAM is more or less the same as standard recording. The only difference being that the digital interface/driver is selected in the Audio Hardware and Drivers window in LAM.

Word Clock

One thing that is very different, however, is a beast called word clock. If there is a problem in this area then you will get clicks, pops and other glitches in your audio stream … or LAM will crash constantly. Either way, this ain't exactly what you're after, I'm sure …

I have kept this as basic as possible, so if you're a propellerhead, please excuse the oversimplification.

The term ›word clock‹ accurately describes what it is and does—a *clock* pulse is transferred for each sample *word*.

When you transfer data digitally between devices, not only is the audio portion of the data sent, but also other coding information which determines (among other things):

- Where each data bit in a sample belongs
- Which channel(s) the sample(s) belong to
- The exact sample rate

Part of this coding information—word clock—ensures that the device *transmitting* the data and the device(s) *receiving* the data are in sync with each other.

In other terms, the word clock signal is similar to a metronome and its job is to make sure that the data timing between devices is the same, so that one unit is not being sent information too quickly/slowly. If this happens, it usually results in clicks, pops, data errors etc.

What Happens if I *don't* use Word Clock?

If you set two devices as *master* to the same sample rate—let's say 44.1 kHz—it's *really* unlikely that both machines will be running at exactly 44,100 samples per second!

One machine may run at 44,100 and the other may run constantly at 44,108 … or worse may fluctuate between 44,050 and 44,150. In either case, as time goes by, they will slowly drift apart resulting in the occasional data bit being dropped … and this means pops and clicks. Depending on your audio material, you may not even notice these glitches, but give it a try with a 1 kHz test tone over five minutes and see what happens.

In a Basic Setup

NB: A common mistake some people make—is to leave your DAT machine on and have LAM derive its sample clock rate from its digital input. This isn't a problem until you want to transfer your data back to the DAT. As LAM is receiving the DAT's clock source and—assuming that your DAT machine automatically detects the incoming sample rate when receiving data digitally—a word clock loop happens. This is likely to cause a range of problems, including crashes.

E. g. between a DAT machine and LAM using an S-P/DIF equipped soundcard—transferring digital audio should be relatively painless provided that:

- You use the *right* sort of cable—75 ohm coaxial. This is a fairly standard video cable but there *is* a difference between something from Radio Shack and something from Apogee. Spend the extra $10 to 20 on a decent cable.

  NB: Many new users make the mistake of using a standard audio cable which has RCA connectors. This will not work, or if it by a freak of nature does, you are almost certainly guaranteed of problems at some stage.
- One device is set to *master* and the other to *slave*. Most devices will automatically detect sample rates etc. from connected devices as soon as they are hooked up or data is sent but some devices need to be *manually* set to external sync.
- When recording digitally with LAM it should be the *slave* device.
- When playing back from LAM it should be the *master* device (i.e. turn off/disable the digital *input*).

A Complex Setup

So, you've got yourself a couple of ADATS, a digital mixing console with the ADAT board, a DAT machine, a CD Player, a sample rate converter, LAM and an ADAT-optical equipped soundcard/box (e.g. MOTU 2408) ... welcome to word clock Hell!

In this scenario, you would probably be best served with a dedicated word clock box/distribution amp. Essentially you need everything clocked from the one source set up in a ›star‹ network.

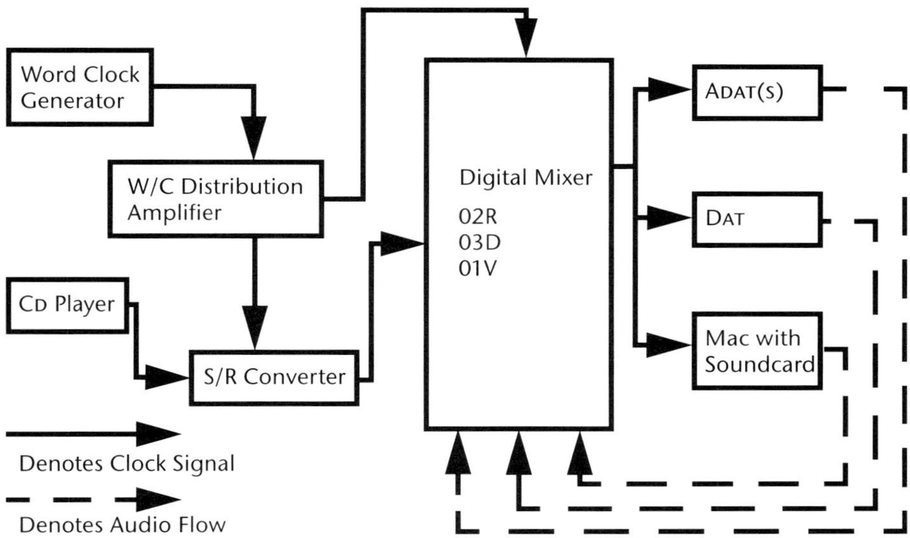

In the diagram, all devices are clocked from the word clock generator via the distribution amp. The reason for the amplifier is more than just acting as a splitter/junction box—digital signals degrade over distance so ›daisy-chaining‹ is out!
The *audio flow* coming from the ADAT/DAT/Macintosh is digital.

As everything is running off a master clock, these devices (and the mixer and sample-rate converter) are always in *slave* mode.

In this example, all devices will run on one master clock signal from the WC generator, so even if it has a sample rate which varies, *all* devices will fluctuate at the same time/rate. This allows (theoretically) perfect lock—i.e. sample-accurate sync—between your devices.

5 Audio Handling and Editing

OK, no more of that hardware, configuration and set up stuff! I'll assume that you've correctly set up your audio hardware and have an audio file of some sort on the hard drive which you're keen to start messing around with a bit. If not, copy the Audio folder from the CD-ROM to your hard disk.

First up, we'll take a look at audio file handling in the Arrange and Audio windows and then move on to some basics about the Sample Editor. Over the ensuing chapters, we'll concentrate on the fun stuff—the Digital Factory, EQs and Effects.

LAM 4 has a new ›Audio‹ menu in the main file menu where you'll find the Sample Editor, hardware setup and Audio window.

OK—Let's get to it!

The Arrange Window

The Arrange window is where you spend most of your time with LAM, and it contains a wealth of facilities for manipulating audio regions, as well as MIDI data. I will make the assumption that you are familiar (at least on a basic level) with the handling of the various Arrange window options.

We'll start of by looking at some facilities which work just like their MIDI counterparts, such as the mute button.

As with MIDI sequences, you can click on the *bottom* left or right hand side of any audio region and while holding the mouse button down, you can drag. This will alter the visible appearance of the audio region, and will also alter the playback, so that *only* the visible portion is actually heard. The cool thing is that your original audio file is unaffected and restoring it is a simple click/drag operation.

NB: When the bottom *left* of an audio region is dragged, it will also adjust the default *anchor* which means that the audio region start point will be out of time/sync.

As an example of this in use, take a look at the picture below.

Track 1 is the original region, track 2 is resized, track 3 is a small segment taken from the regions above and track 4 contains copies of this segment. Working this way, individual snare, hihat or other audio region segments can be copied and placed wherever you wish to accentuate or completely change a rhythmic loop as one example.

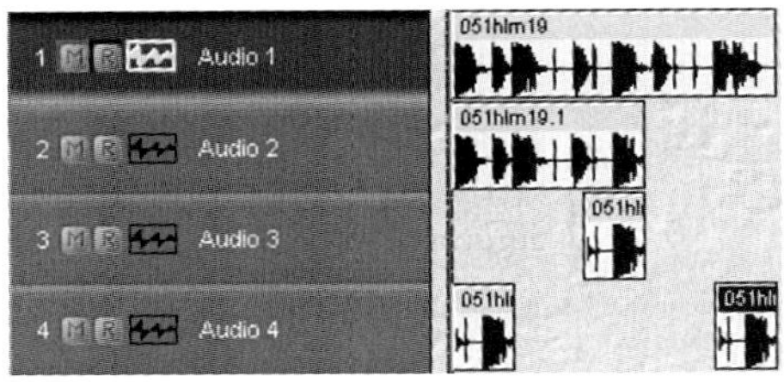

Other options for simple audio manipulation can be found in the part parameters box, including looping, fade in/out and audio playback start delay (which can also be set negatively, starting playback earlier).

Note the diagonal region running through the sample. This is a graphical representation of the audio fade time set in the part parameters box to the left.

Another—considerably more flexible—tool available in the Arrange window is the Cross Fade tool. This tool allows you to fade between two audio regions that occupy the same track. If a crossfade is *not* used, audible playback will simply consist of the first audio region and then the second region, played in turn. This can often result in ›pops‹ and ›clicks‹ or radical volume changes and other artifacts in your audio playback. To do a crossfade, simply select the X-fade tool and click/drag the mouse across the area where the regions overlap.

► If two regions (with no X-fade info) are overlapped on a single track, the region which is ›raised‹ (on top) will have priority and will start/continue playing when the other region is reached by the song position line.

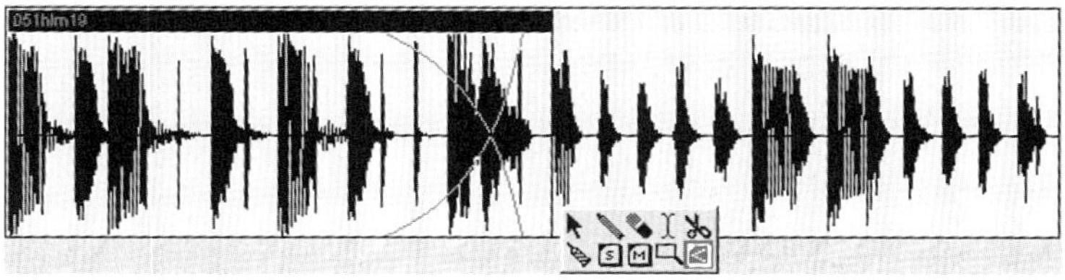

An audio crossfade. Note the X-fade tool which is highlighted in the toolbox and also the curve of the crossfade in the sample display.

By default, crossfades are *linear* which means that they fade one sample in/the other out evenly (at the same rate). In many cases this will be innapropriate. Use the part parameters box to change the curve or alternately, you can globally set a ›default‹ fade time and curve via the Audio Menu > Default Audio Crossfade options.

Another facility for crossfades which you may not be aware of is hidden in the audio region's part parameters box under the word ›OUT.‹ If clicked, a small flip menu will open which allows the selection of different types of crossfades.

- X is a linear crossfade.
- EQP is an ›equal-power‹ crossfade which doesn't place a volume dip in-between the audio regions being crossfaded. This is a much more ›natural‹ sort of crossfade and I highly recommend its use on appropriate audio material.

Handling Loop Repetitions

When using the ›loop‹ parameter on audio regions in the arrange page, the part will cycle over its length until the next object (or region) on the same track is reached. Should there be no subsequent object (or region) on the track, then the audio region will repeat until the song end point is reached. This may or may not be what you're after.

Should you require the region to play for say ... eight bars ... and then be silent for two bars and then restart ... try this.

Select the region and cycle it by clicking beside the ›Loop‹ option in the regions parameters box. A number of gray loop repetitions of the same length as the original audio region will appear onscreen.

At the point (bar/beat) where you would like the audio loop repetitions to stop looping, insert a sequence object which will stop the playback at that point.

From here, you have a choice of creating a copy or an alias of the original region and dragging it to the appropriate position. It is worth noting that any copy/alias of the original object will retain the loop and other parameter settings, but *not* the stop sequence (unless both are selected and copied).

Copies and Aliases

Alias objects/regions are simply pointers to the original region. If any changes are made to the original regions content, the aliases will also be affected, i.e. their content will change in exactly the same way. *Aliases* take up next to no memory, keeping your song files nice and small.

Copies of objects/regions are just that—copies of the original. With audio regions, a new overview will be built and augmented with a number. e.g. ›kickinloop‹ will become ›kickinloop.1.‹ The bonus with copies is that changes to the original regions won't affect them. The downside is that they use more memory than *aliases*.

Independent Track Zooming

A great new feature of version 4 is the ability to view tracks at independent zoom levels. To resize any track (MIDI or audio), simply click to the (bottom) left of the track number in the track list. This will change the cursor to a pointing finger and all you need to do is drag up or down while holding down the mouse button. This facility is extremely useful for a quick visual reference of ›hit points‹ in a sample while sequencing and many other situations.

Audio Window—Tips, Tricks and More ...

Although you can do a great deal of similar audio region and file handling in the Arrange window, the Audio window is where you will do about 90 % of your audio file management and basic ›editing.‹ Outside of the obvious ›Add Audio File/ Save File‹ type of functions which import samples into your song and save them (surprisingly enough!), you can set up loops, anchors and more without the need to enter the Sample Edit window.

File Management

This is part setup task and part rule for working.

LAM allows you to import, play and record audio files to pretty much any folder/hard disk on your system. While this flexibility is a nice thing and allows you to play back multiple audio streams from different hard disks through different sound cards, it also has as much havoc wreaking potential as Godzilla in downtown Tokyo.

When in the Audio File menu > Set Audio Record Path, you can specify where your audio files are recorded for each audio device on your system as shown below.

The Set Audio Record Path window.

Song preparation

My suggestion for a coherent method of working is:

1 In the Finder, create a new folder with the song name.

2 Copy all of the audio files you will (or might) be using (if any) into this folder and copy your Autoload song into this folder as well.
3 Give the Autoload song the same name as the folder.
4 Boot LAW and open the renamed Autoload file from the folder you just created.
5 Open the Set Audio Record Path window and assign your device(s) to the folder(s).
6 Give the files a ›default‹ name which is the same as the song title/folder name.
7 Import any audio files required for the song into the Audio window.

This way your song file and all of your newly recorded (and other) audio files will be in the same place and the new files will all have a related name. In the case of multiple drives/record paths being used, make sure that the file/folder names are the same or similar. If, at a later stage, one of those mysterious ›computer things‹ happen and your audio files disappear, you will be able to track them down more easily with Sherlock.

All of your file management—copy/save/rename/move etc.—should be done *only* in LAM. The exception being archiving which can be done from the desktop provided that *if* you move the *entire folder(s)* to CD-R or whatever, you restore it/them to the same working disk(s) and folder(s) when you want to edit at a later date. This ensures that the file paths (which are saved as part of the song) are correct and LAM won't give you any annoying ›I can't locate the audio file‹ error messages.

How LAM Handles Stereo and Mono Audio Files

LAM 3.5 and upwards handles stereo audio in a different fashion to preceding versions. You will find a number of functions in the File and Edit menus to change stereo to split L & R audio files and vice versa. Below is a rundown on the new audio file definitions and methods of dealing with them.

- ›Mono:‹ Mono regions are played as they are. The left and right side of stereo regions are mixed together to a mono data stream.
- ›Stereo:‹ Mono regions are played as a stereo data stream, left and right contain the same signal. Stereo regions are played as they are. There are basically two types of stereo audio files—Split Stereo and Interleaved Stereo.
- ›Left‹ Mono regions are played as they are. The left signal of a stereo file is played, the right side is ignored.
- ›Right‹ Mono regions are played as they are. The right signal of a stereo file is played, the left side is ignored.

Important: Songs recorded with pre 3.5/3.6 versions are converted with regard to the stereo settings of the samples in the track. Every ›old‹ stereo audio object is set to ›Left‹ and ›Right.‹ LAM will display a dialog box to inform you of a conversion.

The ›Left‹ and ›Right‹ modes are mainly needed to convert older songs with stereo tracks. This ensures that songs created with earlier versions of LAM sound and behave like before. Another reason could be the need to control left and right sides individually.

► The Arrange window can be optimized by using the function: Structure/Track—›Delete redundant audio tracks.‹ It removes the right sides of split stereo files and the track itself.

Split Stereo

The Split Stereo format creates a pair of phase-locked mono files (-L, -R) to carry the information for each channel. This is the format that Logic Audio writes in all 3.0 and earlier versions as well as with versions using DAE.

Stereo Interleaved

All 3.5 (and above) versions that do not use DAE autmatically create interleaved Stereo files. Most CD-R programs use the Interleaved stereo file format, where both channels are carried in a single file.

Converting Split Stereo to Stereo Interleaved

You must convert your older Logic stereo files into the interleaved format for use with such programs. To do this,

1 Open the Audio window.
2 Highlight the desired stereo files.
3 Open the ›Audio File‹ menu and select ›Convert to SDII, AIFF or Wave Stereo‹ dependent on what file type you want to convert to.

An interleaved stereo file with the same name will be written to the folder containing the original split stereo files. Also take a look at Chapter 11 ›Track Bouncing‹ from page 165 onwards.

► Tip: You may find that older song files (pre 3.5/3.6) which contain audio sound ›different‹ when imported into version 4. The reason for this is that stereo files which were previously individual L + R samples have now been combined into a single stereo interleaved object in the Arrange window. It is possible that there may still be a Mono version (either L or R) of the file left on one of the tracks and hidden by the new stereo file. Uncovering and deleting this/these mono file(s) and resaving the song will fix the problem.

Reading Files from CD/CD-ROM

So, you've got yourself one of those audio demo CDs of someone's sampling library and you'd like to use a loop or two in your music. To use info from an audio CD in LAM, you must first convert the CD audio data to AIFF data. MacOs resp. QuickTime features a built-in CD Grabber. Here's how to use it:

1 Open SimpleText from your Macintosh hard disk.
2 From SimpleText's file menu, select open and browse to your CD drive and select the file you wish to use.
3 Press the Convert button.
4 This will open a file save dialog where you can name your file and give it a destination. This window also contains an Options button which allows the selection of different sample rates/stereo mono file types etc.

5 Press save and once converted, you can import the file from the Audio window in LAM.

When it comes to ready-built sample library, stored in AIFF format on CD-ROM (like WIZOO's Hamburg Loopz or Lo-Fi Junkiez) you can import these files using ›Add Audio File‹ in the Audio window. After auditioning these files by clicking on the speaker icon in the Audio Window, simply use the Copy/ Convert Files option in the Audio File menu to save the audio files to hard disk.

In version 4, you may freely drag 'n drop audio regions wherever you please.

► If you wish to edit *any* file from a Read-Only device, you will need to copy the file to hard disk which will change the file(s) attributes.

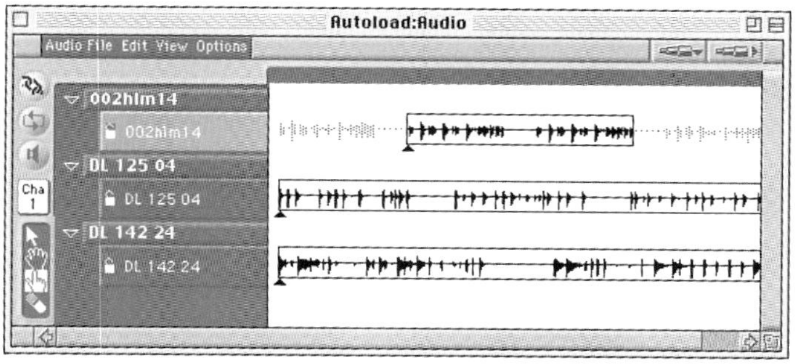

The Audio window

Setting Loop Points

In the picture above, you'll notice that the top file (002hlm14) has just the center of the graphical waveform display (sample overview) highlighted and the remainder grayed-out. Also notice that the cycle/speaker buttons are depressed as this audio file is being looped and auditioned.

If you use the highlighted tool—the finger—on either end of the sample overview, you can adjust the playback region while the audio file is playing. This allows you to set loops over sections of the audio file. When this highlighted region is dragged and dropped into the Arrange window, only the selected portion will play (the Audio Region). The advantage to selecting a region in this fashion is that the original audio file has not been edited, but rather, LAM has been instructed on *how* to play the file—or, more to the point—what section (region) of the file to play.

The ›block‹ which appears once the audio region has been dragged and dropped into the Arrange window will automatically resize to reflect the audio file portion being heard.

While much of this type of audio region resizing can be accomplished in the Arrange window, I suggest the use of the Audio window to do your ›rough‹ edits on your audio files and to set up loops as any opening/saving of files or regions won't require switching between screensets.

If ›Search Zero Crossings‹ is selected in the Edit Menu (should be the default setting) then LAM will automatically ›jump‹ to a value which is most likely to give you a smooth loop when the finger tool is used in the Audio window. This will give you a near perfect loop 90 times out of 100 on the right sort of audio material.

On the odd occasion where you can't get a perfectly smooth loop in the Audio window, simply double-click on the audio region to enter the Sample Editor, but more on this later.

Removing ›Dead Space‹ in the Audio

One of the grooviest functions in LAM is the Strip Silence function found in the Options Menu when in the Audio window. This process has a number of practical uses outlined below.

- When you've read an entire CD-ROM full of loops or other material, the Strip Silence function will separate the one huge sample into small, useable portions—i. e. individual loops/samples.
- You've recorded a vocal or instrument part from beginning to end of the track and the vocalist has paused in between verses, choruses etc. To separate into smaller,

workable chunks, use Strip Silence. It is worth noting that LAM will keep better sync between audio regions when working with smaller samples, rather than long contiguous ones. This is the legacy of audio hardware, bus speed and data throughput issues.

- You have a particularly noisy recording, or someone kicked a microphone stand, dropped a guitar, stick etc., you can occasionally use Strip Silence to isolate and delete the offending portion.
- You can also ›recycle‹ drumloops by using Strip Silence. With the resulting regions, you can do things like: change the song tempo, seperate the individual segments onto separate audio tracks for different Fx processing and mixing. This way, you can give an old loop a whole new lease on life and maybe get a few more songs out of it.

recycle—Some nifty processing on this ›recycled‹ drum loop. Mess around with the tempo.

Strip Silence does not change the content of the original audio file, but rather, creates a set of new regions ignoring silent parts within the audio file.

Once you've processed your audio file with the Strip Silence function, you can then use the ›Optimize File(s)‹ function from the File menu to reclaim disk space wasted by silent portions in your original audio file(s). This may, at some point, save the day in a recording session, but be aware that this is a *destructive* process that will change the original audio file. My recommendation is to use the ›Save Region As‹ function and to change the default of 1,000 ms (1 second) added either side of the newly-created file to zero.

Another major bonus of working this way is that your smaller audio files will be opened and altered *much* more quickly when you use the sample editor or any of the Digital Factory functions and the original file will still be there if things go wrong.

Sample Editor—Tips and Tricks

LAM's Sample Edit window incorporates a *true* stereo editor. What this means is that any connected stereo files will be edited on *both* sides, unless specifically told not to. To illustrate why this is important—imagine a stereo audio file that is five seconds long. If you were to cut out the section between seconds 3 and 4 and then butt the two ends up together, you would be left with an audio file that was four seconds long. If this type of edit only happened to the left side of a stereo file and the right side was untouched, then the two sides of the file would be of different lengths and seriously ›out of whack‹ with one another.

Note that if you add an effect to one side of a split stereo audio file—particularly one with a ›tail‹—reverb/delay etc. you *will* change the file length which will make rejoining the left and right sides an ugly proposition.

In general, you should use the default stereo file handling of LAM and edit both sides of your audio files together, but if you need to edit/effect just one side you should write down the specific sample numbers for your cut points etc. so that this same region can be altered on the other channel of the file (if you intend on using it later).

While I personally prefer to use the Audio window for looping and the ›Save Region As‹ function to create new smaller audio files, you can also use the Sample Editor's Create New Region or Selection ⇨ Region functions to do the same job.

For those of you who ›live‹ in the Arrange window, you can do the same thing here by using the Export region as audio file function.

The advantage of the Sample Edit window over the Audio or Arrange windows is its precision. It simply allows a far closer look at, and therefore edits of, your audio files.

The disadvantage is that this precision can also develop the most carefree individual's anal retentive side. It is *very* easy to spend hours getting a bunch of audio regions ›perfect‹—and then forgetting what you were going to do musically with them. It's entirely up to you, but I suggest the ›rough and ready‹ Audio/Arrange window approach to get your ideas down and then polish in the Sample Editor after the fact. There are, of course, certain audio files that will *have* to be doctored in the Sample Editor, but many won't.

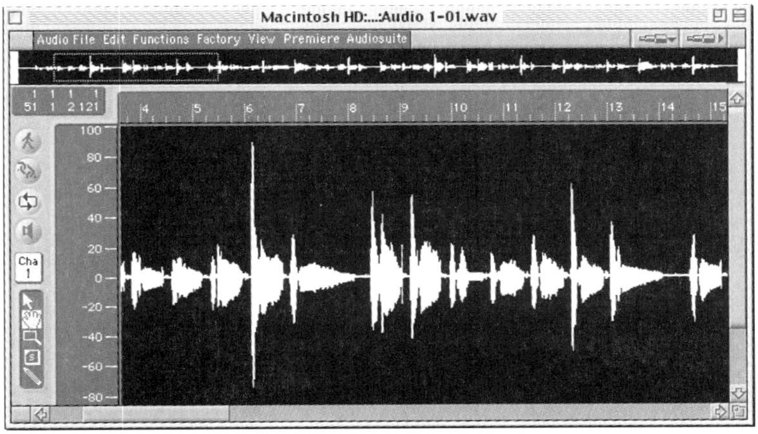

The Sample Editor

The Functions Menu

The Functions menu is where most of the ›standard‹ audio processing tools are found which allow you to reverse, normalize audio files and regions etc. etc. The manual covers what they do and their use, so I won't repeat this, but rather I'll just cover some things that you should keep in the back of your mind when using these tools.

In the Settings under the Functions menu in the Sample Editor you can select the peak level for normalizing. Should you apply Normalizing prior to the final stage of your mixdown, select 90 to 94% as this allows some headroom for EQing later if necessary.

- **Normalizing** is the process of raising the level of an audio file to its maximum without introducing distortion. To do this, the peak (loudest) point of the sample is identified and its distance from the maximum possible level is calculated. With this figure, the entire selected region is increased by this amount. You should be aware, though, that normalizing of signals can introduce quantization noise (›grainy‹ sounding) to your signal. This is not going to be an issue initially, but the potential for the appearance of these unpleasant artifacts is likely to be multiplied by successive digital operations like the use of Fx or EQs. Apart from this, the audio file may well be amplified anyway by the use of EQing or Fx. As *the* preferred method—be sure to use an optimal recording level and use normalizing as the final step after all other editing processes (this includes Fx) have happened.

- **Fade in/out** time is controlled by the Settings option in the Functions menu and offers a range of fade curve types. Linear isn't always the best choice.
- **Remove Dc Offset** is useful for many Macintosh owners. When a signal is recorded the onscreen waveform display should be ›centered‹ on the horizontal line. If it isn't, you can correct the electrical symmetry using Dc Offset.

► The Sample Editor—in fact *all* of LAM's 90 screensets—have three ›variations‹ for Zoom settings. These are not set by default, but should you wish to do so, you can open the Key Commands window and find ›zoom.‹ Look for ›Save as‹ and ›Recall‹ Zoom 1, 2 and 3. Set up appropriate keys/commands and you'll then have instant access to various detail levels when editing your samples. Trust me, this facility saves hours.

The Pen(cil) is Mightier than the S-word

Version 4 (finally) brings a new addition to the tools in the Sample Editor—the pencil.

NB: Use the pencil tool for little cosmetic changes within one waveform cycle rather than for any ›sound design‹ visions you may have—LAM contains far more effective options for the latter.

The pencil tool allows you to do small cosmetic changes manually by drawing directly into the waveform. This comes in handy for repairing clicks in a vinyl recording or ultra-short spikes from a hard disk failure.

Typically, you would approach the trouble spot using the scrub function, then zoom in on the waveform overview in the Sample Editor until the spike was visible.

Following this, you can even out the waveform using the pencil, and the spot should be repaired without any audible artifacts.

The next stop in our tour of the Sample Editor deserved its own chapter—the Digital Factory—so, let's get to it!

6 The Digital Factory

This chapter covers some ›destructive‹ sound manipulation options found in the Digital Factory. You should be aware that many of the Digital Factory functions actually make changes to your audio files. This type of processing is called ›destructive‹ editing.

It is also worth noting that many of these options are now possible (in real time and non-destructively) using the new Fx plug-ins contained in version 4.

Time and Pitch Machine

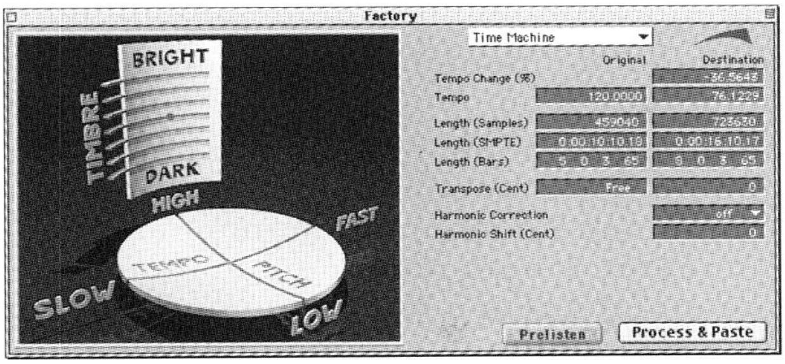

The Time and Pitch Machine can be used to create some funky tempo and pitch changes over the course of an audio region. Many users simply adjust the whole audio file/region but there's nothing to stop you from selecting a portion of it and altering just that section. Below, you'll find some creative time and pitch based manipulation options for you to try, but first, I'd like to explain some of the things that you should know. These will help you make the most of the Time and Pitch Machine.

- A semitone step is broken down into 100 ›cents,‹ so therefore if you wanted to transpose an audio file up/down three semitones, you would adjust it by 300 cents up (sharp—higher in pitch) or down (flat—lower in pitch), an octave 1,200 cents a. s. o.
- By default, the Time and Pitch Machine is in ›Free‹ mode, which allows independent adjustment of pitch and length. If you want that ›Mickey Mouse‹ or ›Darth Vader‹ thing, switch to ›Classic‹ mode which will lock sample length and pitch together, meaning that as you adjust pitch, the sample length will change and vice versa.
- You can use the Time and Pitch Machine on stereo samples, but don't try to adjust stereo files by more than an octave as all sorts of artifacts may creep into your sound. I find that changes by a third/fifth up to a seventh work best.
- Avoid pitch shifting on drum loops or tracks that contain drum material. Why? Basically because it makes the individual drums sound ›artificial.‹ Time stretching on percussive material stirs up the transients, making the sound ›greasy‹ and ›punchy.‹ Time stretching on rhythmic material can also affect the inherent timing of the audio file and make the drum loop sound ›all over the place.‹

Tip: Double-click on any of the value fields and type in your numbers directly when using any of the Digital Factory tools. Using the mouse to grab balls, dots or as a slider is a waste of time and simply not accurate enough.

► Tip: A much better option for altering the tempo of a drum loop is to chop up the loop into single beats using the Strip Silence function (see page 94). This will leave you with a collection of audio regions which will automatically follow the song tempo, provided the original audio region was in the Arrange window at the time the Strip Silence was done and you answered ›yes‹ when asked if you would like to ›replace.‹

Time and Pitch Machine ›Tricks‹

- If you adjust the (cent) value in the Harmonic Shift field but not in the Transpose field, the Time and Pitch Machine will *generate* harmonic content which doesn't exist in the original audio file allowing you to ›fatten up‹ or ›brighten‹ the sound, without adjusting the pitch or length of the file. Harmonic Correction needs to be On for this to work.

- Apart from obvious uses like fixing flat or sharp notes, you can do wild pitch changes that break up your audio file for that really ›grungy‹ or just plain ›weird‹ sound.
- On a four-bar vocal audio file, the first bar could play back at normal pitch, second bar could play back at twice the pitch, third at four times etc. Given a bit of delay, under real-time control, this could create a really interesting (and trippy) option. (Think Babylon Zoo—›Spaceman‹)

◎ Trippy—Tempo tricks with the TPM

- You've probably thought of pitch shifting your audio files to create harmony vocal tracks, but more on an ›all or nothing‹ basis. Why not chop up your audio files (in the SE or using Strip Silence) and use time-stretched and pitch shifted regions of it as your harmonies. As an example, let's cut up ›Row, row, row your boat.‹ One part will be ›Row your boat‹ which can be time stretched to match the length of the original sample and then pitch shifted up a third/fifth or whatever. What you end up with here is ›Row, row, row your boat‹ with a ›Roooow—youuuur—boaaaat‹ harmony part above it.
- To figure out how far to adjust the tempo of your audio file when using time stretching for loop matching, follow these steps:

1. First, you should edit the audio file so you're left with an Audio region which is of the right length, loops properly etc.
2. Once this is done, open the Arrange window and select the audio region you want to match the tempo of.
3. Set a loop region appropriate to the region and in the Options/ Tempo, select ›Adjust tempo using object length and locators‹ and when prompted click on ›Globally.‹
4. At this point, look at your transport bar's tempo indicator and write this value down, including *all* of the numbers after the decimal point.

5 Repeat steps 2 thru 4 for your second audio region.
6 Reset the song tempo back to the first regions' value and open the second region in the sample editor.
7 Select the Time and Pitch Machine from the Factory menu and insert the tempo value of the first region in the Destination Tempo field. Ensure that no pitch shifts etc. are set up elsewhere in the TPM.
8 Process your audio file—make a backup when asked—and you're done!

Audio Energizer

The Audio Energizer

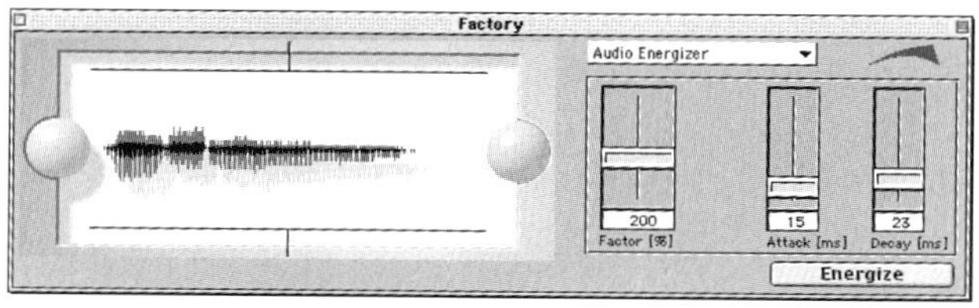

The Audio Energizer has been made somewhat superfluous by the compression, distortion and other Fx in version 4, but it can be used to create a kind of compressed, yet overdriven effect and have it integrated (processed destructively) into the audio file. It can also sound sorta like tape saturation.

Energy—Drum and Bass loop given the ›treatment‹

The best way for you to get a handle on what it's capable of is to load up a drum plus bass loop and mess with the parameters, particularly the attack and decay. Try settings of 100, 48 & 76, running from left to right, which will give you a musically useful result. Get more extreme if you like but make sure that you create a backup of your original audio file as this is a destructive process.

It is worth noting that setting the Factor parameter over 200 starts to mess with the dynamics and general health of normalized audio files. This may be just the ticket for those of you who find aircraft and jackhammer noise ›soothing,‹ but as this value increases, so does the amount of time it takes to process the file. You could be waiting a long time to hear the result, and it may not be what you were after anyway.

The Silencer

Next is the *Silencer* which is great for gutting the body and upper mids of a sound, but still leaving a few behind. It can be used as the software equivalent of the world's worst engineer going nuts with EQs and can really make things sound bad—which may be good—with the right bit of music.

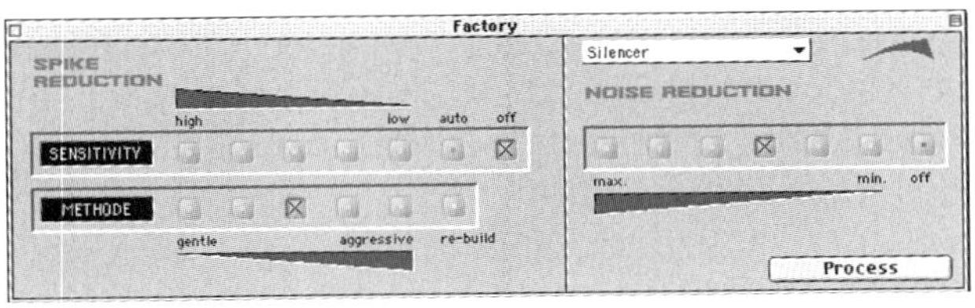

In general, you should use fairly conservative settings (i.e. lower values) for each process. If your audio file actually *needs* aggressive processing then it's probably too far gone and should be re-recorded. Alternately, it can be left alone and you should change your approach and go for a ›retro‹ (read ›dirty‹) feel/sound on your track.

If you really want to mess with your audio, try the Rebuild function which analyzes audio file data on either side of what the Silencer perceives as a ›spike‹ (loud bit) and generates synthetic material. This is great for destroying a drum loop and the result can be recycled via Strip Silence and reused to underpin the original audio file (i.e. play back your messed-up version alongside the original) for anyone doing ›nasty‹ grooves.

Destroy—this snippet of audio gets taken out into the back alley and has the crap kicked out of it by the rebuild function.

To be honest, the Spectral Gate does all of this plus so much more ... and I recommend its use (big time) over the Silencer unless you need to destructively change your audio file.

The Groove Machine

Straitlace and Swunglace. A hip-hop groove is actually made straighter with the regroove function.

This utility allows you to make a straight groove ›swing‹ (or vice-versa) and is covered in great detail by the manual. Emagic's recommendation is that you use this when the audio file's tempo matches the song tempo. In 99 % of cases, this is true but there's nothing to stop you from doing something ›wrong‹ with your audio file (i.e. processing it at the wrong tempo) and then using the loop matching technique discussed earlier in the Time and Pitch Machine section or the Strip Silence function in the Audio window on ›Removing ›Dead Space‹ in the Audio‹ on page 94.

Strip Silence will break up your processed audio file into smaller regions dependent on how the threshold is set. These can then be deleted, moved or edited as you would with any other audio region.

Tip: Use the Sample Editor's Create New Region or Selection ⇨ Region functions to grab a section for regrooving.

The bottom line here is that while the regroove of the *entire* audio file may not work, parts of it may be perfect, particularly when used in conjunction with the original loop.

Audio to MIDI Groove and Back!

a2midgrv

I won't go into details with how the Audio to MIDI Groove and Quantize Engine applets work, but I'd like you to consider this.

The ›Audio to MIDI Groove‹ function analyzes audio data and creates a MIDI ›feel‹ template based on the peaks and troughs in the file. This template will then become available as an option in the Quantize menus found throughout LAM's various edit windows.

The ›Quantize Engine‹ reads these templates and applies them to audio files. Ergo, using these two Digital Factory tools in conjunction allows you to take the ›feel‹ of one audio file and apply it to another.

This is perfect for people like me who are hopeless guitar players. I can record a couple of bars of suspect funk guitar, analyze the original I was trying to emulate from the ›artist formerly known as‹ or JB and apply this feel to my ›white boy‹ playing.

That's about it for this chapter. Next up—LAM's Audio Mixer.

7 Fx Routing and Mixing

Among the coolest features of LAM 3.0 and up are the internal CPU-based software effects. To facilitate the use of these, Emagic devised an extremely flexible routing arrangement to circumvent processing power issues and also to give musicians a method of working familiar to most of us—that of a hardware mixing console. This has been extended further in LAM 4.

Throughout this, and the following chapters, we'll look at how this ›virtual mixer‹ works and some methods and shortcuts for making the most of your (possibly) limited hardware resources.

The choice and control of effects have been *greatly* enhanced with version 4. There are a number of all-new algorithms, which sound better and offer vast potential which simply wasn't possible without a stack of third-party plug-ins in former versions. It is now possible to do an entire mix, using only LAM's internal Fx.

It's worth noting that LAM 4 is far more efficient with its overall CPU usage than previous versions ... which basically means more tracks and effects can be used simultaneously.

Effects Bussing

The LAM mixer features up to sixteen (in LAM Platinum) effects ›busses.‹

You can activate pop-up menus that are located under Send in each channel strip to select one (or more) of these eight effects busses you want to route the signal to. As you're not limited to a single Send bus, it's possible to route any given audio channel to multiple busses, and therefore, multiple effects in a parallel or series configuration.

LAM 4 also allows the redirecting of the individual Returns (busses) to other busses, allowing a staggering number of submixing possibilities.

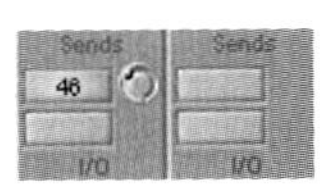

Once the audio has been routed to a bus by selecting an option from the Send flip menu, a Send knob will automatically appear on the selected channel strip. This knob controls the level of signal being sent to the bus.

Each of the Send busses on each channel features an option to send the signal Pre or Post fader. Note that the Pre and Post options are only available in the Send flip-menu *after* you have assigned a Send bus.

So, What's the Difference between Pre and Post Modes?

- Post-Fader: the Send signal is routed out after (Post) the channel fader, so if you pull the channel fader all the way down, the Send level will also be zero.
- Pre-Fader: the Send signal is routed out before (Pre) the channel fader. In this case, the level of Send amount is controlled solely by the Send knob.

In Post-Fader mode the direct signal (the Dry signal that is controlled by the channel fader) and the effects signal (called Wet in audio speak) are joined at the hip. This is usually the desired configuration, so Post-Fader is considered to be the ›standard‹ operating mode.

In Pre-Fader mode, if the channel fader is pulled all the way down, none of the dry signal is audible. You'll *only* hear the wet effects signal. You can change the amount of wet signal level independent of the dry signal by using the Send knob.

So Why Would You Want to Use Busses?

The advantages of sending your individual audio channels to the eight busses are:

- You may want several instrument/vocal parts to be routed through the same type of effect(s), particularly if the effect has a timed or rhythmic quality to it.—Flange sweep/vibrato, delays etc.

- You may want to route your audio through different busses in a parallel Fx configuration, but more on this later.
- With multiple audio channels sharing a given bus, the CPU only has to generate one effect for many tracks to be able to utilize it. This is particularly useful if you don't have a state-of-the-art Macintosh sitting in the studio … or even if you do and are using a high-end third party effect that is a resource pig.
- Even when *not* using the Fx, routing multiple audio tracks through one bus allows you to combine all of the tracks into a single mono or stereo sample using bouncing which we'll discuss in Chapter 11 from page 165 onwards.

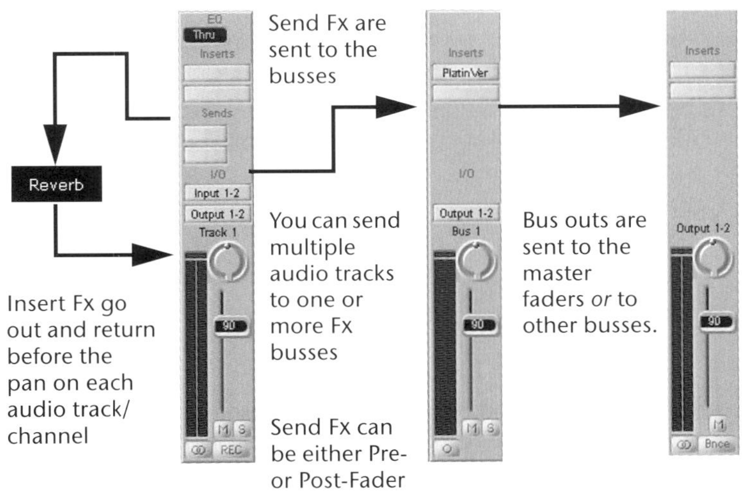

The Send and Insert effects signal flow

Insert Effects

The bus channel strips lack the EQ and Send of individual channels, but the FX plug-in scheme works in exactly the same fashion as Inserts on individual tracks, so this information can be applied here as well.

As an alternative to routing signals to effects busses via Sends, you can use the Channel Inserts. Here, the signal chain is cut, the dry signal is routed through one or more effects devices, and the wet signal is spliced back into the signal path.

Eight Inserts are available on every mono or stereo channel, affording up to 512 (Wow!) Insert effects in an Audiowerk equipped Macintosh. (Star Trek's Enterprise computer will be needed for 512 Fx, however!) This is in addition to the four EQs on each channel and the 128 possible Bus effects in Platinum. Further to this, are an additional eight Fx on each Master Output.

NB: Insert effects happen *after* the channel EQs in the signal path, so if your EQs are active, they will affect the overall tone of the signal before it reaches the effect(s).

The output signal of the final Insert effect is routed back to the channel prior to the Pan control.

- The advantage of Insert effects is that you can have a specific effect (or combination of effects) on a particular audio channel strip, allowing precise sonic control. The downside is that each Insert effect takes an amount of the CPU's resources, which, in the real world, means that a handful of tracks will be swimming in Fx—the rest will be as naked as the day they were born.

Send or Insert—When and Why?

So, which type of effects routing scheme is best for which purpose and why?

Send

Using Sends, you can route as many channel signals through any single (or multiple) effects bus(ses) as you like. This is pretty handy when you're using seriously CPU-hungry plug-ins (read ›third-party‹). Sends are best (and usually) used for effects which are ›added‹ to the signal—like reverb, delay, chorus or flanger.

You can also use sends to sub-group particular instrument families (drums, strings etc.) to simplify the task of mixing fade-outs etc.

Insert

This is the type of effect routing you should use when you *don't* want to mix the wet effects signal to the dry signal, but would rather Insert (hence the name) the Fx signal into the direct signal path.

The most commonly used Insert Fx are dynamics processors (compressors, gates, limiters) or signal processors like EQs or filters.

Serial and Parallel Effects Setup

In a *Series Configuration* the output from one effect is summed with its incoming signal and fed into the input of the next effect in a chain

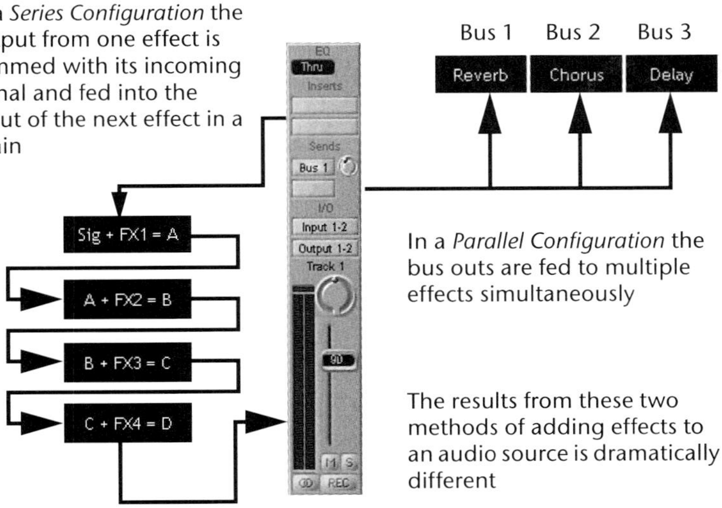

In a *Parallel Configuration* the bus outs are fed to multiple effects simultaneously

The results from these two methods of adding effects to an audio source is dramatically different

As individual audio channels can be sent to multiple busses, you can use these busses in a parallel effects configuration.

You can set up effects in series on a single bus which work exactly like the Inserts on a single channel. This way, you can route multiple audio channels through one bus with a particular serial effects combination, saving both time setting 'em up and CPU resources.

Use your Insert effects in a series effects configuration. This type of flexibility allows you to combine different effects in different ways so that you can build your own complex multi-effects.

Take a look at the diagram for both series and parallel Fx routings above.

It's possible to use several effects on a single audio signal even if you don't have a Cray supercomputer by using the ›Bnce‹ button on the Master faders. We'll take a deeper look at this in Chapter 11 from page 165 onwards.

Fx Routing—The Big Picture

LAM features a window which allows you to get a complete overview of what's really going on with your mix. This is found under the Audio Menu > Audio Configuration.

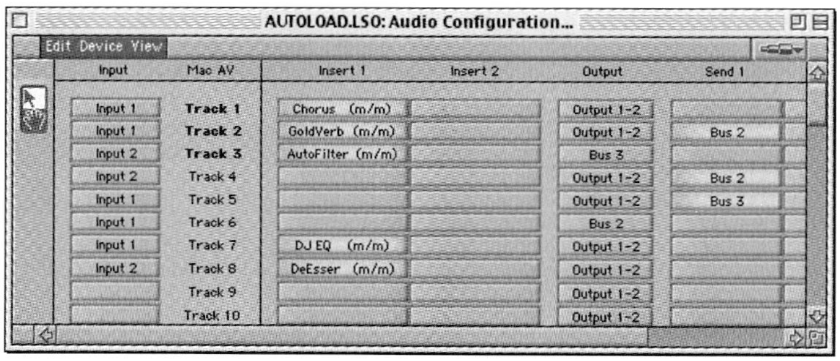

My suggestion is to set up a screenset with this window, your audio mixer and a System Performance meter. Should you find that your system is ›glitching‹ (or crashing), you'll be able to use this screenset to enable/disable Fx and track down the resource hog quickly. Another plus is that scrolling from side to side in the mixer can be avoided, making setup faster and easier ... particularly with the 64 faders and 16 busses in V 4.

The Track Mixer

The Track Mixer window only contains the audio or instrument objects that are visible in the track list in the Arrange window. It also includes related objects that *aren't* in the track list like the first two busses (which is a bummer if you want to use more) and the first master fader (channels 1 and 2—which is somewhat useless if you're using a multi I/O card and are using different outs) for the audio objects. For this reason, I don't recommend its use and suggest that you use the Audio layer in the Environment.

Another limitation of the Track Mixer is in its handling of MIDI objects. In this instance, it sets up a default GM set of adjustable parameters (Fx depth etc.) which is again useless on a non-GM device.

The only user I could recommend the use of the track mixer to would be someone using the Macintosh's internal sound hardware with QuickTime Musical Instruments.

8 Automix—LAM Style

LAM's Environment allows you to create full-on mixes with both MIDI and audio data using a couple of different techniques.

First of all, LAM's internal mixer is a full-on Total Recall console. You can—at any given time—change to a different project and return later to continue your work exactly from where you left it, recalling volumes, EQ and Fx settings with a single mouse click.

The term ›automation‹ refers to the recording (and playback) of the movement of faders, pots etc. in real time—which is, imaginatively, referred to as Real-time automation—and also the capturing of ›Snapshots‹ which is known as Snapshot automation (bet that comes as a surprise).

Which method you prefer to use is up to you, but in some cases your hardware will make the choice for you, as delays in audio mix automation data are commonplace. This latency (there's that word again) between the audio mix data being sent and the audio actually being affected is caused by things like soundcard processing issues, drivers and system configuration problems.

If possible, within your mix, route ›fixed‹ tracks (tracks that don't require level adjustments throughout the song) to a single (or a couple of) bus fader(s). This allows you to quickly mute/adjust the volume of many tracks with a single mouse movement or key command which is handy for fade in/outs and also for dropping the general mix volume when making fine adjustments to other tracks.

Real-time Automation

You can automate parameters using dynamic events by simply selecting the Audio Mix track (or the audio objects' track itself), dropping into record and moving faders onscreen.

Alternately, you can use Hyperdraw—my strongest recommendation—to do the same job but with a couple of important differences.

- It's more precise than moving faders with a mouse.

- The controller data is integrated with the audio region so when (and if) you move or copy the sample to another location, the mix information remains with it.

Depending on your system's latency, you might find that there's a delay between what you see and what you hear in HyperDraw, so you may need to reposition the events— your best bet is the event list editor for its ability to precisely move a single (or multiple) selection of events—until the results sound good.

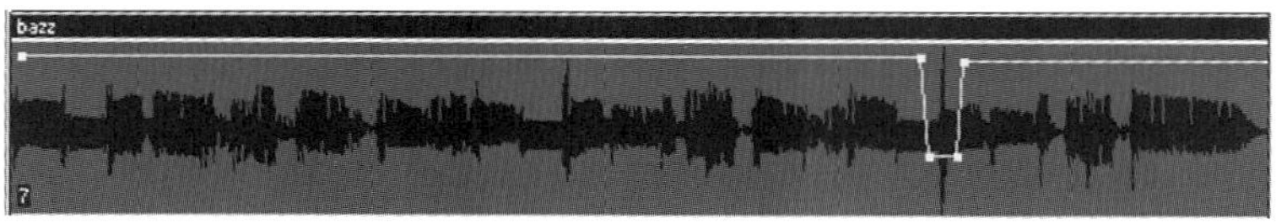

By drawing volume control curves, you can decrease the level of overly loud signals in your audio files and achieve an effect similar to compression or gating.

Snapshot Automation

Automation in hardware mixing consoles like the ProMix, 02R and others, works by setting up a static automation Snapshot and then adding dynamic elements to the mix after the fact. In many cases, this method of mix automation works well in LAM.

A Snapshot refers to basic fader and pot settings that are switched ›hard‹ (as opposed to a gradual or gliding fade from one setting to the next) at different points in the song. So how do you set up Snapshots? ... Here's one method ...

(◎) Snapshot. Here both snapshot and dynamic automation are used on this drumloop track.

1 First up, select the Audio Mix (A-Playback) object in the tracklist in your Arrange window.
2 In the Arrange window create a blank sequence object.
3 Extend the sequence out to match the length of the sample you want to ›mix,‹ by clicking on the right hand end of the ›block‹ until the cursor changes to a double-headed arrow and then dragging it to the right.
4 Press the Pause and Record buttons on your transport bar.

5 Move the Song Position Line to the spot that you want to insert your ›snapshot.‹
6 Adjust your faders, pots etc. in the Audio Mixer.
7 Repeat steps 5 and 6 for extra Snapshots.
8 When you're done, press Stop on the transport bar. Return to the beginning and play it back.

To add any fades and real-time stuff after you have set up your Snapshots I would, as mentioned, suggest the use of HyperDraw on individual tracks.

You can, of course, also use the various ›Send Fader‹ options within the Audio layer in the Environment (or the Adaptive Mixer window) at particular points in the song, either with or without the pause button enabled, but I prefer the method above. It's a bit more ›hands-on‹ and while far more labor intensive, generally delivers a more precise mix. Another point is that all snapshot mix information from *all* tracks is in the one place (i.e. on one track). This allows easier editing later on if necessary.

► In the Audio layer of the Environment, you'll find a Mixer Automation submenu under Options. This allows you to select the type of mix automation you want for your edits. *Be careful* with this as ›Replace‹ mode will destroy all of your previous mixer edits. Use one of the other modes.

Which Parameters Can Be Automated?

To be honest—everything you can think of and more can be automated in Logic—basically every fader, knob or switch that is related to a mixer object.

This includes obvious parameters like volume, pan or mute status as well as not so obvious stuff like EQ or even the internal Fx.

► Version 4 includes a vast range of excellent built-in plug-in Fx, and each parameter of each plug-in can be automated. This is not always the case with third-party plug-ins—see their documentation for info about automation facilities.

Dreaming of the flanger speed changing over time, the song fading out with a closing synth filter or distortion becoming heavier in the solo part? Here you go!

The Zen of Automation

LAM's mixer automation, as mentioned earlier, can not only be used for volume and pan changes, but also for control of EQ and effects parameters in real time which can really give that ›pro‹ edge to your productions.

Rhythmic EQ, pan and effects manipulations can also deliver some really ›bent‹ results as well, so experiment!

statEQ—A drum loop, EQ'ed bigtime

- Play back the loop in Cycle mode and listen to the obvious EQ settings.
- Delete the automation track and set up your own.
- Use static or dynamic automation to activate these settings rhythmically.

dumbEQ—The same loop with stupid amounts of automation—a classic *don't* do this example.

- Use buttons such as EQ ON/OFF rather than continuous controls. This generates a lot less data, wreaks less havoc on the timing and is much easier to edit later on.
- Play back the automated sequence and check out the results.

Fixing the Mix

If you have a ›pretty close‹ to final mix, simply use the Event List for those final ›tweaks‹ to make things perfect:

1. Select the appropriate audio track or audio mix sequence and open the Event editor.
2. The Length/Info column will tell you what type of data you're dealing with.
3. You can delete, move or quantize any data as per usual with a MIDI track. By varying the Num Column values, you can also change the data type. As a simple example you could convert an EQ ON message to an EQ OFF message after the fact… it's your call.

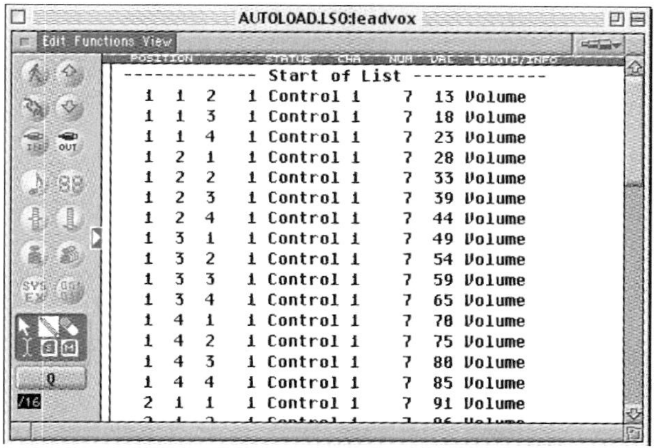

Don't forget your simple cut/copy paste tools either. If one track in the mix already has something similar to what you need, use this data and minimize your editing.

► Tip: *Always* make a song copy (preferably numbered—song1, song2, song3 etc.) *before* you try to automate your mixes. This way, you've always got a backup to return to if things go wrong (and they will, sooner or later). LAM 4 can be set to automatically back up your data at predefined intervals (Options > Settings > Global Preferences, I suggest setting this to the last two to five mixes at most (I personally turn it OFF) or you could end up with hundreds of versions and no hard disk space for further recording.

9 Equalizers

Now that we've had a look at the mixer as a whole, I'd like to focus on the individual channel strips within the mixer. First off:

The EQs

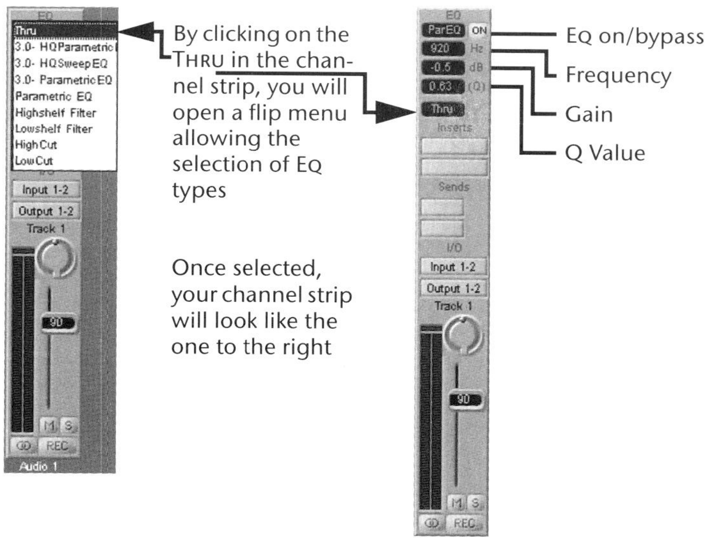

Note the Thru which appears on the right hand image below the various EQ parameters. Use this to select up to four separate EQ bands.

Many people—particularly new users—simply view LAM's EQ as something to boost a bit of bass or treble here and there. For more experienced hands, EQs both in the software and in hardware units, are *much* more than this.

In fact, if used creatively, EQ can give you options which are simply impossible using any other audio processing tool.

So What Exactly Is Equalization?

The following sections will introduce you to the fundamentals and some ›rules‹ of thumb. Please feel free to break them every now and then as there are many ways to skin the proverbial cat.(My apologies to cat lovers everywhere.)

Equalization (EQ) is the process of boosting or cutting certain frequencies in an audio signal. The name originally came from the process of trying to obtain a flat frequency response—›no coloration‹ or an ›equalized‹ signal. Early pioneers were telephone companies who experimented with EQ to make voices sound more natural over phone lines. In a recording situation, EQ is used to make individual instruments or frequencies stand out (or the reverse) in an overall mix.

Parametric EQs Explained

LAM's EQ section comprises four ›parametric‹ (or other) equalizers per channel.

A single parametric EQ allows you to adjust the amount of boost or cut and define the center frequency and the bandwidth of a certain frequency band. With experience and practice, you can learn:

- where to apply some boost (›peak‹ filter) to help an instrument cut through the mix or achieve a ›fatter‹ sound,
- where to cut (›notch‹ filtering) to eliminate feedback, 50 or 60 Hz hum and other undesirable artifacts.

Frequency: This control determines the center frequency of the band in Hz or kHz values.

Gain: Also known as ›Presence/Absence‹ or ›Cut/Boost.‹ This parameter determines the extent to which you can attenuate (cut) or amplify (boost) a frequency band; usually the value is expressed in dB. At a gain value of ›0,‹ the filter doesn't audibly influence the signal.

Q-Factor: To minimize the filter's effect on the rest of the sound, you can use a small bandwidth. The Q-Factor (Q =

quality) determines this. The greater the Q-Factor value is, the narrower the filter band.

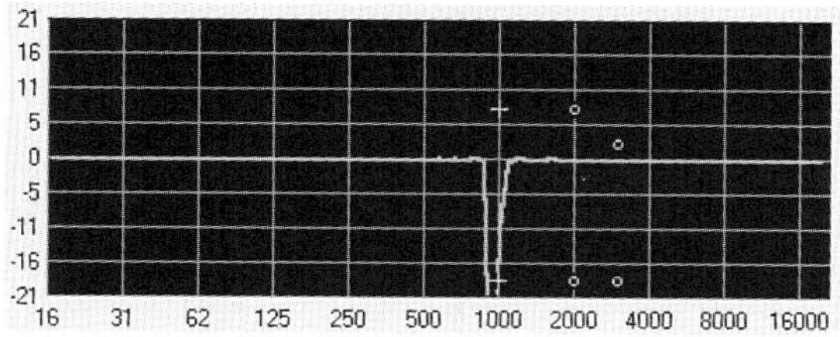

A parametric filter band is cut using a ›notch‹ in the frequency characteristic.

Some extra info about LAM's EQ that's worth knowing is that each EQ uses an amount of processing power, so figuring out just how many EQs you can use simultaneously is determined by your computer's performance specs, the number of other effects being used and the selected EQ quality.

EQs—Stereo or Mono?

You needn't worry about stereo or mono channel issues. If you're tweaking the EQ of a stereo channel, both sides of the signal are automatically affected. Logic-ally, EQs on stereo channels require more computing power.

► However, you can use any EQ as an Insert effect rather than in the EQ section. In this case the Stereo/Mono routing conventions described on page 138 apply.

The Right EQ for the Job

LAM allows you to select from a range of EQ types which are of a higher quality than the version 3.0 EQs. As LAM 4 retains the version 3 EQs for compatibility with older song files, I have also included brief descriptions of these types of EQs in the following section. So what exactly does each one do to your sound and what application should each be used for?

LAM 4 retains the version 3 EQs for compatibility with songs created in earlier versions. These EQs are not selectable in version 4.

Parametric EQ

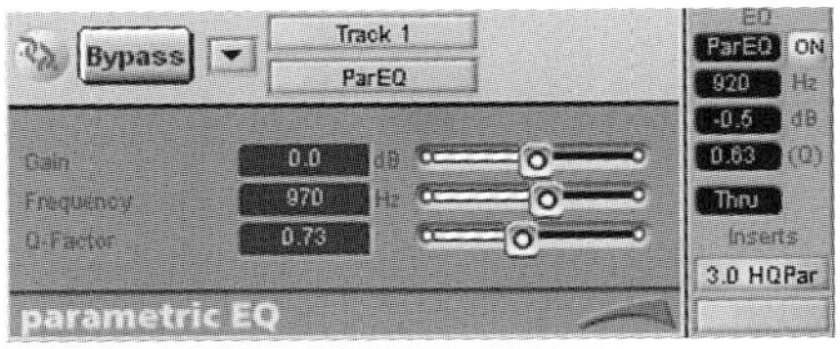

Both versions of the parametric EQ are shown here—as a plug-in and as one of the four bands on the channel strip.

This EQ is more precise than the ›standard‹ Parametric EQ; its phase response is more accurate, so clarity and transparency are enhanced substantially. Use this EQ type when you're mixing acoustic instruments, vocals or mastering a complete mixdown. It is more CPU intensive than its lo-fi equivalent.

Sweepable EQ

A ›sweepable‹ EQ is essentially a parametric EQ with a fixed Q factor of 1.0 and therefore without a Q control. It uses less CPU power while still offering the clarity and precision of the high quality Parametric.

Low Pass

A Low pass filter allows frequencies *below* a certain value to ›pass,‹ thus cutting the range above the Frequency value. Its function is comparable to that of a statically set Lowpass filter in a synthesizer. Unlike a parametric EQ, there is no gain parameter—cutoff frequency and Q (slope) are the only variables.

Also unlike the parametric EQ which creates a bell-like notch in the frequency curve, Lowpass is used for damping the entire high frequency range above a certain point but leaving the lower range alone. The Q factor controls the steepness of the filter—4 being the steepest curve.

In the plug-in version the steepness can be switched using the Pole parameter—a value of 1 gives you a more natural filter shape, while a value of 2 audibly cuts the signal.

High Pass

High pass is exactly the opposite of Low pass—it cuts the low frequency range. You can use it for thinning out signals that interfere with say, the bass track or the kick drum.

Low Shelving/High Shelving

A low shelving EQ—unlike a Low pass filter—can either attenuate or raise the frequency range below the chosen frequency value. If you set a negative gain value, it acts like a High pass filter but gives you a much more flexible Q control.

Use the Low Shelving filter to boost the whole frequency range below a certain point. This adds ›balls‹ to any signal.

You can use it as an alternative to the High Pass filter if you need more accurate control over the slope of the filter.

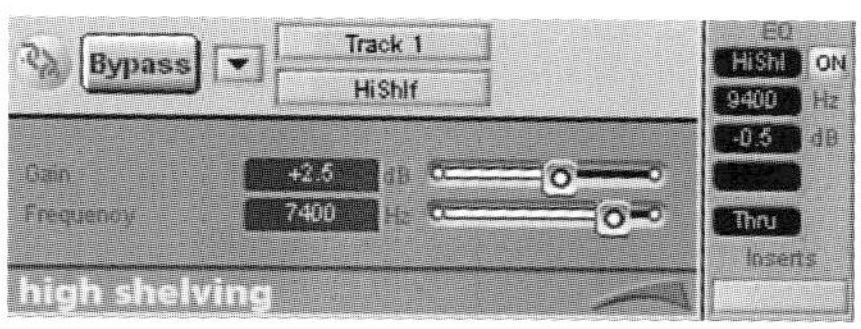

Hi Shelving is exactly the opposite of Low Shelving. Use it to boost the entire frequency range above a certain point. This is useful e.g. for cymbals as well as vocals.

► In hardware mixers Low Pass/High Pass filters and Shelving EQs are typically located at the outer limits of the frequency range, with one or two parametric EQs in between. While you have completely free choice of EQ placement in LAM, I recommend you adopt this method as it simply makes sense.

EQ Handling

If you run into CPU-related bottlenecks, use ›Track Bouncing‹ to save the EQed signals to individual audio files. Once you have set up the optimum filter settings, export them one after the other.

So, how do you actually handle an EQ? Simply change the values? In principle yes, but it's essential that you know where, why and in which order you should ›tweak‹ your settings.

In this respect, hardware mixers have an advantage over their software counterparts. In fully parametric EQs, all three parameters are normally assigned to separate knobs. Most people can manipulate two controls at once, and more ›gifted‹ individuals can deal with three or more simultaneously. (They're the ones from ›close‹ families who have a finger for each string on a banjo—or a harp!)

Needless to say, you don't have that direct, tactile connection with LAM so you need to employ a different technique. Here's one that I like:

I generally use EQ to cut frequencies rather than boosting. This is, of course, completely dependent on the piece of music, but cutting with EQ helps keep the integrity of any stereo imaging and phase correllation/ balance etc. between tracks. Boosting with EQ can sometimes screw this up, so just keep it in mind.

1. Try to identify the frequency range using the ›sledgehammer‹ technique. To do this, start with a radical gain setting of 20 dB and a Q value of approx. 8 using the HQ parametric.
2. Now ›tune‹ the EQ, using the mouse as a slider in the Frequency window. Do this slowly and listen closely for the position where the EQ first audibly influences the frequency you're looking for and where the EQ stops affecting it. The best value for the frequency parameter is smack in the middle of these two outer limits.
3. Once you've located the frequency, you can change the Gain and Q settings until you get what you came for.

► In order to set parameters precisely, simply double-click on the number you want to change and type in the new value using your computer's numeric keypad. LAM will automatically ›round off‹ the number to the closest possible value.

All about Frequency Ranges

First off, we'll refresh your math skills to gain a better understanding of the numeric relationship of frequencies. The golden rule is: ›The musical interval of one octave above (up an octave) is equal to twice the frequency of the octave below.‹ Read on, it'll make more sense, I promise:

Frequencies 101

An ascending octave from A at 220 Hz leads up to concert-pitch A at 440 Hz. Way up there in the ›Kate Bush‹ register, you'll find another A at 7,040 Hz (7.04 kHz). To find the next ascending A, you again double the frequency to 14,080 Hz (14.08 kHz). In this example, the octave between the two low A's is only an interval of 220 Hz, the octave between the two high A's a whopping 7,040 Hz!

What this means when you're EQing is that a slight deviation of the frequency parameter by just a few Hertz in the bottom end has a significant effect. If you boost a bass frequency somewhere around 60 Hz or 100 Hz, you'll notice a huge difference.

On the other hand, when you're working with higher frequencies and you set a frequency parameter of 14,000 Hz to 14,040 Hz, no one (other than your dog) will hear the difference. With treble frequencies, you have to think big, so use larger ›steps‹ in this range.

The lower the frequencies that you want to manipulate, the smaller the frequency increments should be.

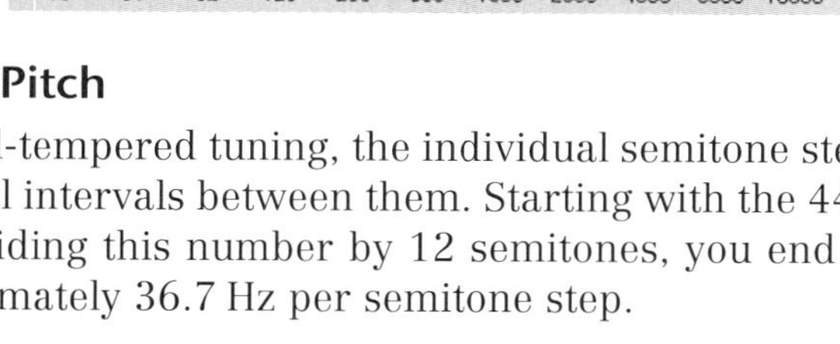

Take note of the frequency ranges along the bottom of the diagram. This shows the relative scale of the frequency spectrum

About Pitch

In equal-tempered tuning, the individual semitone steps have identical intervals between them. Starting with the 440-Hz A, and dividing this number by 12 semitones, you end up with approximately 36.7 Hz per semitone step.

Here are the frequencies for a major triad with a root at concert-pitch A and another A an octave higher:

- A = 440 Hz
- C# = 4 semitones higher = 440 Hz + 4 × 36.7 Hz = 586.7 Hz,
- E = 7 semitones higher = 440 Hz + 7 × 36.7 Hz = 696.7 Hz
- A = an octave higher = double the original frequency = 880 Hz.

Don't bother about learning all of the tones and their frequency equivalents to thirteen places after the decimal point. It won't get you your studio engineers cap, membership card and secret decoder ring. Just keep the basic principle in the back of your mind as it will help you to design sounds and eliminate unwanted frequencies.

Sinchrd—A descending major triad with an added octave and a concert-pitch root played in sine tones.

1. Open the song file and play track 1.
2. Mute track one and unmute track 2.
3. Using the formula discussed above to calculate the frequencies: The lowest tone has a frequency of 220 Hz, the highest 440 Hz.

► Another key point is that (for you math geniuses) the three semitones above 220 Hz would equal 330.1 Hz and 7 semitones above would equal 476.9 Hz. So why are the values set to 270 Hz (275.05 actually) and 350 Hz (348.45)?

The answer lies in the fact that each octave interval *doubles* in frequency going up—so logically—it must halve coming down. To calculate your semitone steps (36.7) between pitches you *must* adjust this accordingly.

In this example you should work with relatively narrow frequency bands—i. e. a higher Q-Factor—so you don't address all of the tones at once. You'll note that in the song file, the Q-Factor has been set to 24 (it uses the ver 3.0 EQ, hence the Q value above 10), which as you'll discover, is not what you want to do when dealing with ›natural‹ sounds. EQing is, unfortunately, not nearly this easy in the real-world and you'll find it considerably more difficult to isolate individual tones with EQ in more ›musical‹ or natural sounds.

The Q-Factor—Shaken, Not Stirred

All sounds that occur in nature (or elsewhere) are actually combinations of Sine tones (also called ›Root‹ tones) plus their related Harmonics. Pure sine tones contain no additional harmonics whereas all other types of sounds do. The root tone determines the pitch and the harmonic structure determines the timbre or tonal color. The brighter or livelier a sound, the greater its harmonic (overtone) content. Obviously, if a sound is chock-full of harmonics, it will be all over the place in the frequency spectrum. This has the following ramifications when you're selecting a suitable Q-Factor:

- High Q Values, 8 to 10 (14 to 24): Extremely narrow filter bands destroy the natural balance between the root tone and overtones. In most cases, this type of EQ will make acoustic instruments and vocals sound artificial. Extremely high Q values are used for a drastic ›fix‹ in the mix—for example to kill feedback in a live recording or to create weird effects.

Q values in brackets refer to the Version 3.0 EQ

- Middle Q Values, 4 to 7 (5 to 14): This range comes in handy when you want to alter the individual aspects of a sound. e. g. to accentuate the low-end rumble, fat mids or silky highs when you're mixing a cello sound.
- Low Q Values, 0.5 to 4 (0.5 to 5): You should use relatively wide filter bands for global EQing tasks such as ›beefing it up a bit‹ or ›adding a little sparkle.‹ You'll notice that changes made in this range are more subtle because the original timbre remains pretty much intact. The result is usually more pleasing and somewhat more ›musical.‹

For normal tonal corrections, you'll find that relatively low Q parameter values between 0.5 and 2.5 will generally deliver the best results.

To get a feel for how different Q values sound in combination with various Gain and frequency settings, mess around with the following example for a while.

EQ1—A groovy loop

1 On Track 1 thru 4 of EQ1, you'll find two-bar sequences of a drum loop from WIZOO's Hamburg Loopz CD. Focus on the timbre or tonal color of the sequence.
2 Mute Track 1 and listen to the EQed sequences on Tracks 2, 3 and 4. Switch Track 1 back on and experiment with the loop via an EQ band.
3 Note how different Q and frequency values have a different effect on the tonal color.

As you can see, even with just a single filter band, EQing is no easy task. With practice, you'll be able to do similar tasks using two or more filter bands.

► An EQ doesn't magically conjure up frequencies, it simply changes existing ones. In other words, you can only EQ a frequency range if it's actually present in the audio material that you're dealing with.

Creative EQing

An EQ is a pretty handy little tool which can be used for much more than just ironing out the bugs in an audio recording. It's also a creative option in LAM's bag of tricks. The following section discusses a few of the more unusual EQ applications.

Sound Design via EQ

HiHat—A hi-hat track is a ›noisy‹ sound that is ripe for radical EQ settings to achieve weird effects.

1 First, listen to the original version of the hi-hat loop and then turn on the bands in the EQ, one by one.
2 The frequencies are tuned in octaves, which gives you an interesting mix of tonal and noisy characteristics.
3 Mess with the frequency and Gain settings.

Experiment with other noisy sounds. With narrow-band filters, you can emphasize individual frequencies so that they leap out of the mix.

Balancing Levels via EQ

1 First listen to the drum loop and then turn on the bypassed EQs.

2 Try to set up an EQ setting that captures the conga drum so that you can attenuate it without affecting other frequencies in the loop. Vary the EQ parameters and note the different effects.

3 While you're at it, why don't you try to eliminate the conga from the mix. The frequency around 300 Hz will get most of it, but use the other bands to zap more.

4 Add another conga to the mix in the desired groove, e.g. by playing it on a MIDI sound generating device.

◎ lathat—A latin-ish drum loop that would be great for a song, if only the congas sounded different.

This type of manipulation rarely sounds ›perfect,‹ but when heard in conjunction with other signals (e. g. when you overdub a new kick drum or bass later on), it often does the trick.

Separating Tracks via EQ

This example takes the previous example a step further. It's definitely more advanced and demonstrates a technique that will let you set up some pretty wild effects:

1 First listen to the drum loop and then turn on the bypassed EQs.

2 The EQs are set so that the kick drum is more audible in one track and the hi-hat in the other. Swap them by using the channel Pan controls.

3 Experiment more with these to ›fine tune‹ them. I have deliberately left them rough. The end goal is to get as close as possible to just kick on one side and hihat on the other.

◎ LrEQ—EQ separation

Generating Pseudo Stereo via EQ

1 For both tracks, activate all four frequency bands with a medium Q value. Spread the frequency parameters of the four bands relatively wide (e.g. 400 Hz, 1 kHz, 2.5 kHz and 6 kHz).

2 Boost the first and third band and cut the second and fourth band in one channel. Set up the opposite EQ Gain configuration in the other channel.

3 Set one channel's Pan to the far left, the other far right.

◎ String—Mono strings that might sound better in stereo ...

Your result should be a ›pseudo stereo‹ sound which will be fuller sounding, particularly when monitoring through headphones or mediocre speakers.

► Over the top EQing is more effective when you limit yourself to individual components in the mix. As an example, if you ›monster‹ a hi-hat, it's usually a good idea to add another ›normal‹ hi-hat that plays a different groove to the other side of the mix, otherwise the effect will sound artificial or somewhat strained.

An Overview of the Frequency Ranges

Human hearing is very sensitive, but it's certainly not perfect and no two people have exactly the same equipment. You'll detect some frequency ranges readily, whereas others have to be ›in your face‹ before you take note of them. This difference between people's auditory systems is known as ›subjective hearing‹—where one individual may hear a particular frequency that another person is oblivious to. To close out the EQ section, we'll take a quick tour through the more prominent ranges of the frequency spectrum (i. e. ranges that most of us hear):

20 Hz to 60 Hz

Sub-bass with ultra-low frequencies is hip; techno-heads and ravers especially enjoy frequencies low and loud enough to cause heart attacks. When working with these frequencies, you need gear that's capable of reproducing heavy-duty bottom end rumble like special subwoofers normally only found in large PA systems ... So, unless you happen to have one lying around the house, go easy on these frequencies. One exception is when you're doing ›dance‹ remixes and have to ›pump up da bass.‹ Another factor in ultra-low land is that the majority of instruments and microphones simply won't give you the kind of ›oomph‹ you're after, so you'll probably need to invest in special Fx devices or plug-ins (sub-bass generators).

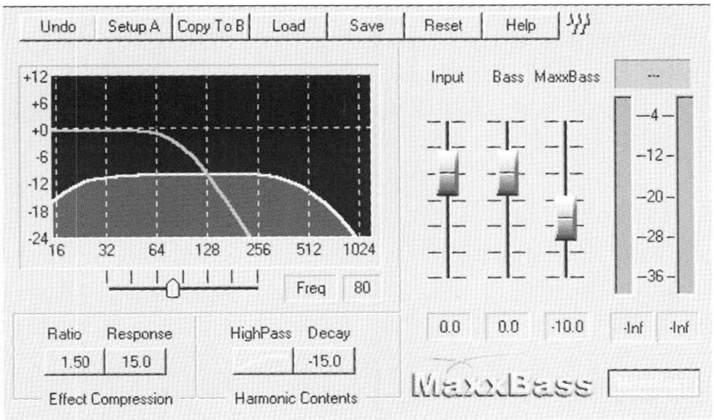

The MaxxBass sub-generator plug-in from Waves can add those ultra-low signals to the mix.

60 Hz to 100 Hz

Even in many high-end hardware mixing consoles, 60 Hz is the EQs bottom limit, and with good reason. This is low enough for virtually every musical style other than the newer electronic stuff. As discussed earlier, the range between 60 and 100 Hz is very sensitive and is where you normally ›tune‹ the bass. Be careful when you're EQing the bottom end and choose the sweet spot, i. e. where the bass signal delivers the biggest punch and the least mud.

As usual, there's a drawback: You won't hear much of a difference until you invest in a good (usually = expensive) set of monitors. When you're working with small nearfield monitors, the only thing that will help you out is experience. Try different settings while mixing and jot down notes on each EQ configuration. Listen to your mixes through larger speakers, a car stereo and, if at all possible, a large PA system. This is the only way that you'll get a ›feel‹ for what the bass EQ should sound like on your tiny monitor speakers so that your mixes deliver the goods over other sound systems.

100 Hz to 200 Hz

This is the range where bass and low mids meet and is a cool starting point for tweaks to bass signals. As an example, if you've recorded a really low, rumbling bass line, you should position the kick drum a bit higher in the frequency spectrum—somewhere between 120 Hz and 160 Hz is usually a good spot.

200 Hz to 1 kHz

You'll find that the ›mid-range‹ is the frequency zone that is definitely the biggest challenge during mixdown. It really is difficult to get a handle on, so your best bet is to leave it alone unless you're having a *major* problem with the composite mix.

If your mix sounds ›muddy‹ and ›cluttered,‹ which often happens when you record under difficult conditions (live) or use low-quality gear, then your recording is probably chock-full of mids. Even the cheapest dictaphone or answering machine records these. If other frequencies such as ultra-low basses and high-resolution highs are missing it's probably because they weren't recorded in the first place. Listen to the different tracks, identify those with an inordinate amount of mids and try to cut these frequencies.

If you've ended up with loads of bottom end punch, but the entire recording sounds cold or artificial, try applying a bunch of low mids to make the mix sound warmer and more natural.

In contrast to the problem above, an absence of mids is most often caused by going overboard while EQing the tracks.

The quality for which these frequencies are known is best described as ›warmth.‹ This range is crucial to vocals and electric guitars. If your vocal take lacks mids, the voices will sound cold and synthetic. If the guitar track is light-on for mids, you'll end up with an excellent electric razor sample for your library, especially if you used a DI box rather than miked an amp. If you run into this type of problem, subtly boost the frequencies somewhere in the range of 300 Hz to warm it up.

1 kHz to 3 kHz

Our hearing is especially sensitive to this frequency range and, like no other, it has the capacity to give you that ›fingernails on a blackboard‹ shiver. If you find that a signal is too cutting or ›edgy,‹ cut the frequencies in the 1- to 2-kHz range. In almost every case, this will fix the mix. On the other hand, if you're too severe in this region, you'll end up with aural cotton wool.

3 kHz to 12 kHz

This is the frequency range normally associated with the high-end or ›treble.‹ Here you shouldn't be attempting to capture entire instruments, you should rather concentrate on those parts of the signal that lend the sound some ›sparkle.‹ If a guitar sounds dead or your vocalist *soundssss like thisssss*, you can fix these problems in this frequency range.

12 kHz to 20 kHz

This is where we start getting into ›for your dog's enjoyment only‹ territory. The higher you go, the brighter and shinier the highs. At the same time, you're pushing the limits of human hearing and what speaker systems can reproduce.

If your mixdown lacks sheen or sparkle, boost these frequencies. 12 kHz is a good place to start, moving up in frequencies as the situation dictates. Again, you can only boost what is actually there. Ride cymbals, vocals and some synth sounds are best-served by these upper end frequencies.

► The best example of the ›ideally EQed‹ CD is your favorite song, and, because you're so familiar with it, this is also the best exercise material you can use to train your ears for your own mixes. See what happens when you boost or cut the different frequency ranges on this track. Try doing the same thing with all kinds of audio material—it's definitely worth the effort and your future mixes will benefit from your new ›smarter‹ ears.

10 About LAM's Plug-ins

The proliferation of digital audio recording software over the last couple of years has seen the emergence of the VST API as a ›standard‹ for *realtime* plug-ins. As a result, a vast range of LAM-compatible effects plug-ins are available.

The list is huge and would easily fill a guide of its own (see below for more about this). On the CD-ROM included with this book, you'll find a motherlode of info and demo plug-ins for you to experiment with in LAM.

LAM also supports plug-ins in Premiere and Audiosuite format, but these are *not* realtime processes and they destructively alter the audio file when applied. These types of plugins are only available in the Sample Edit window, not in LAM's audio mixer.

Although Premiere and Audiosuite plug-ins have a number of shortcomings, there are many unique effects which are *only* available in these formats, so you shouldn't completely write them off.

► And now for a different kind of ›plug.‹ WIZOO has a guide to VST and VST plug-ins, which will give you an insight into hundreds of effects. Take a look in the back of the guide or at the catalog on the CD-ROM for more info.

Enough of that for now though. Let's take a look at LAM's internal effects and then close the chapter by looking at a few setup issues regarding their use.

► There will be a dedicated WIZOO book for Logics internal FX as well. ›Logic 4 FX Collection‹ will be available in fall 1999. The accompanying CD-ROM will feature a complete FX library of 500 ready-for-use EQ- and FX-Presets for sound design, processing and mastering. This library of professionally created presets for each plug-in gives you countless creative options and makes the effective use of Logic's FX a piece of cake.

Stereo/Mono Plug-in routing

Before we start, I'd just like to cover a little thing which many LAM users may not be aware of. Many plug-ins come in two or three versions. Their *visible* difference is the appendix of the plug-in name in the flip menu, the *audible* difference is much more significant:

Obviously the s/s plugs need more CPU power than the others, so make sure not to waste them on mono signals.

- ›s/s:‹ Stereo in, stereo out (True stereo). Both input signals are processed separately, so the stereo qualities of the signal remain unchanged—this is most obviously important for summed or stereo bus signals used as inserts.
- ›m/m:‹ This is a full-on Mono version—Mono in, Mono out. Be sure to use it on mono signals *only*. Typical applications are EQs or dynamic processors as mono inserts (Kick, Snare, Bass).
- ›m/s:‹ Mono in/Stereo out. For use with mono signals only, but the effect output is stereo. Use this for typical stereo effects that are applied to mono signals: Chorus for bass, Reverb for lead vocal.

► IMPORTANT!!!—Version 4 of LAM automatically limits the available FX types shown in the flip menus on the audio objects to match the audio objects signal I/O settings. In other words, if an audio object is mono, then *only* mono (and mono/stereo) FX will be available in the plug-in flip menu. This also applies to stereo audio objects with *only* stereo plug-ins being available.

It is possible to override these settings by pressing and holding ⌥ before selecting the plug-in flip menu on an audio object. This may prove useful if an effect is only available in a mono or stereo version.

NB: If you choose to use a plug-in which does *not* match the audio objects' signal I/O flow, LAM will be forced to do a data stream conversion which requires more CPU resources, so keep this in mind.

Loading/Saving Presets

Some new things you'll find in version 4 of LAM, outside of the all-new algorithms and Fx interfaces, is the ability to save/load effects presets libraries, which is accessible in each effect via the downwards-pointing arrow beside the Bypass button. This opens a flip-menu which shows a range of functions. Not only can you save/load presets for LAM's internal Fx, but also for third-party Fx. A nice inclusion which was previously unavailable.

Version 4 automatically creates a folder called ›Plug-in Settings‹ and within this, a separate folder for each effect when you first use the save/load preset functions in this flip menu. These folders are then used by LAM to keep track of your Fx settings and, because all of your Autofilter or Platinumverb etc. settings are in their own folders, you should find it easy to keep things under control if you go berserk and create hundreds of presets.

This auto folder creation feature also happens with VST effects, so if you have a lot of third-party plugs, you're gonna have a lot of folders in LAM's install directory.

Reassigning Plug-in Windows

Instead of opening a separate plug-in window for every effect on every channel—which would involve a lot of effort and require a 500-inch monitor—you can reassign any open plug-in window in two different ways using the two flip menus to the upper right of the editor window:

Both options save you a lot of time and give you a much better overview, specifically in complex mixer set-ups.

- Using the upper flipmenu (typically showing a channel name) you can switch the editor window between all channels using this specific plug-in. E.g. if you have applied the Silver EQ to tracks 1/2 and 3/4, you can switch between these channels and adjust their EQ parameters.

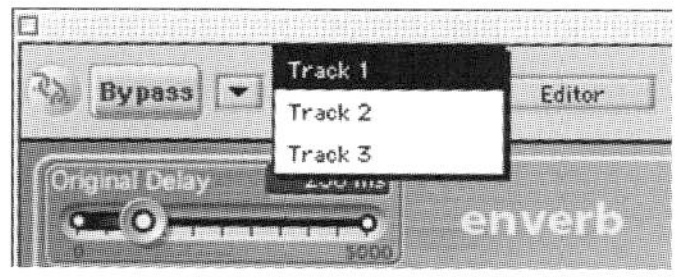

- In the lower flipmenu you can switch between the plug-ins selected for that specific channel. E.g. if one channel uses a Chorus and a Reverb plug, you can switch the window between them.

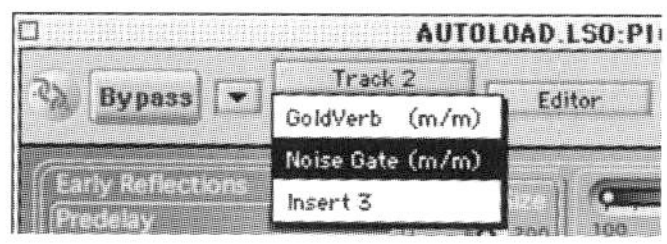

Changing Plug-in Display

Another thing you'll find in many—although not all—of the Fx is an ›Editor‹ button which allows you to switch between the sexy new graphical look and the ›Controls‹ look (horizontal faders) of version 3.x. The ›controls‹ look usually gives you a better overview and is handy if you need to save space onscreen.

Time to take a closer look at LAM's new and exciting range of onboard plug-ins:

EQs

These are essentially the same as those mentioned in the EQ section, but can be inserted at any point in the signal path as opposed to *before* the effects. What this means is that you can filter the sound further if you find that a Flanger, Chorus or another effect has introduced transients or sonic artifacts into the sound.

New to version 4 are the filter Fx. These are essentially extended versions of the EQ section and include the Fat EQ, Silver EQ and DJ EQ, in descending order regarding functionality and CPU usage.

- The Fat EQ is a full-on multi-band EQ (five bands) and is indeed ›phat‹ in the sense of being luxurious. Each band has a switchable characteristic and can be individually turned on/off. As this EQ offers supreme functionality combined with high CPU power consumption, I'd recommend its use for sophisticated processing of vocals or other prominent tracks in the mix. It is also the first choice for final mastering.
- Silver EQ is a very common and power-saving combination of both Lo/Hi-Shelving EQs with a parametric mid EQ in between—exactly the kind of EQ you'd find on most semi-professional hardware consoles. It's quickly set up, easy to use and does the job for most average applications.
- The DJ EQ is similar to the Silver EQ, except that the Low/Hi shelving frequencies cannot be changed. An obvious

application is simple, effective adapting of imported drum loops to the overall mix.

AutoFilter

autofilter

Also included among the ›filters‹ is the AutoFilter. This is, however, no simple EQ but rather a true Synthesizer low pass filter with a load of luxury options.

Besides the usual cutoff and resonance controls there are a lot of fancy options making it a truly outstanding sound shaping tool rather than a plain vanilla Cutoff/Resonance control:

- The Fatness parameter can compensate for the ›thin-out‹ effect that high resonance values have on the signal. Use it when you want to use resonance but keep the ›balls‹ of the input signal. Don't use it if you want the resonance to cut like a knife.
- The AutoFilter includes a full-on ADSR envelope. Everytime the input signal level exceeds the threshold, the envelope is triggered and modulates the Cutoff frequency—this is the ›Auto.‹ The Modulation slider beside the envelope controls the depth of this modulation. There's also a Dynamic Mod control. The higher the value set here, the deeper the impact of the signal level on the

envelope depth. This is, technically speaking, an Envelope Follower function, but when compared to a synthesizer it works kinda like a Velocity Depth parameter.

- The filter works in Low pass mode only, but there are four choices for the filter slope/steepness. The higher the value, the sharper the filter blade cuts the signal, leaving less of the frequency range above the cutoff frequency.
- In addition, or alternately, to the envelope you can use the LFO to modulate the Cutoff frequency. It offers five waveforms including random. If you select the pulse wave, you can control the pulse width (the relation of on and off phases) of the LFO modulation using the Pulsewidth control.
- As another unusual option there's a Speed Mod control. Whenever the level of the input signal exceeds the Threshold, this value is added to the LFO frequency value. In plain English: Signal peaks make the LFO faster.
- There are two distortion options: Input and Output. Input distortion is useful for applying ›amp simulation‹ characteristics as the distorted signal gets filtered post (after) the distortion stage. The Output distortion is more useful on hardcore techno sounds because you can also distort filter sweeps—e.g. distorting resonance sweeps can make a classical flute sound scream like a chainsaw.

This is a *way* cool effect that you will have fun with for weeks, hacking and butchering anything and everything from drum loops to guitars to vocals.

Chorus Effects

Chorus is traditionally used to ›fatten‹ or ›thicken‹ a sound. It is commonly used on electric pianos, guitars, synth sounds in general, leads etc. It works by generating a modulated delay that sounds slightly out of tune with the source signal.

The result is comparable to the sound of two oscillators detuned, except that depth and rate of the modulation can be controlled more accurately in a chorus effect. There are two types in LAM 4.

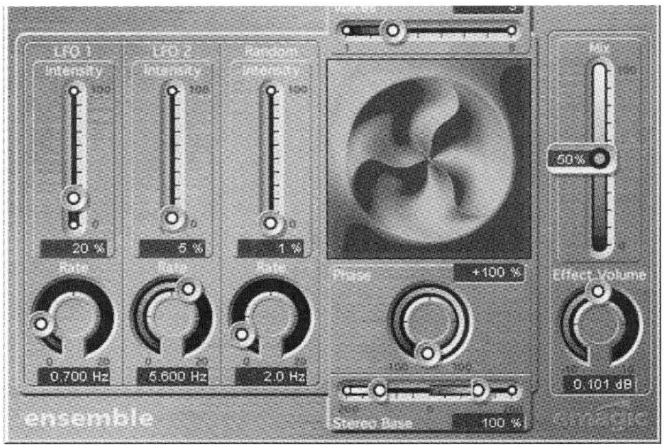

ensemble

The second of which—Ensemble—offers far more control over the effect including the ability to adjust time (modulation phases) in fine increments between ›voices‹ and control over the number (up to eight) of ›voices‹—i.e. independent effect signals—it generates.

Flanger

flanger

Flanging is a different type of modulated delay.

The main difference between the Chorus and Flanger is that the Flanger feeds the effect signal back to the Flanger Input (Feedback). The higher the Feedback amount, the more cutting the Flanger sound appears. The resulting comb filter sounds great on percussive sounds like electric pianos, clavinets, percussive synth sounds. At slow modulation rates it adds a spacy quality to drums, pads, atmospheres and stereo mixes.

Phaser

phaser

The phaser shifts the phase of signal transients which offers a different kind of cyclic modulation. Unlike the Chorus or Flanger it really changes the sound character if applied heavily.

Its impact on the overall tonal color comes close to formant filtering, i.e. the sound sometimes sounds like changing vowels.

LAM 4's phaser offers a couple of cool features which set it apart from other soft and hardware phase shifters. Among these are:

- two mixable LFOS, with mod rate controllable by the input signal level as well.
- sweep ceiling and floor adjustable individually instead of a simple center frequency and modulation depth.
- stereo phase can be swept thru 360 degrees which effectively allows you to change the phase relationship between stereo channels.

Phaser is typically used on string ensemble sounds, basses, e-pianos and guitars. It adds a certain psychedelic quality to a range of signals.

Delays

The LAM delay algorithms offer really precise control over the timing of your delays, which is ideal for sequenced or arpeggiated material that may require perfect synchronicity between the original and effected signal. Delays can be used on pretty much any type of sound.

Let's go through them …

Tape Delay

tapedelay

The tape delay imitates the sound of old, analog tape echoes. The LAM version, however, is much more sophisticated. It automatically knows the current song tempo, so syncing your delay times to the beat is a no-brainer. Basically you just need to select the appropriate note value—crotchet, triplet etc.—and Bob's your aunties' live-in-lover. If you want to take this a step further, you can use the ›groove‹ function to adjust the selected note value to a dotted crotchet/triplet … this is particularly handy if you're using one of the ›swing‹ quantize (16A, B, C etc.) values on accompanying MIDI tracks or if the audio file is actually a bounced MIDI track that used a swing quantize.

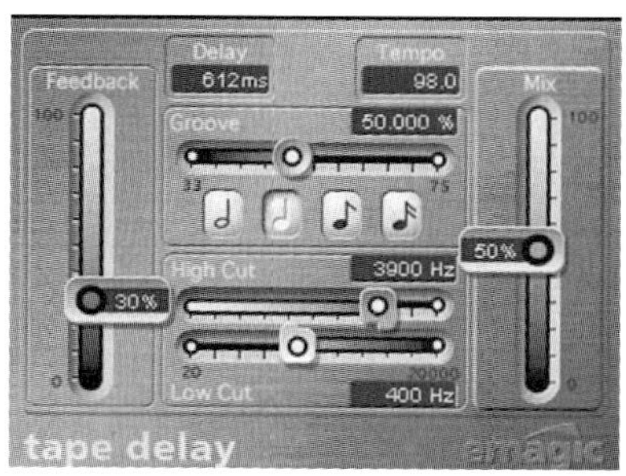

The feedback parameter—apart from setting the number of repetitions—also simulates tape saturation. This truly simulates the behaviour of analog tape echoes—i.e. the signal quality getting a bit worse and losing brilliance with every repetition.

Stereo Delay

Surprisingly light on the computing power required due to the absence of the feedback/tape saturation parameter found in the Tape Delay. Has independently adjustable crossfeed allowing the left/right channels to have subsequent delays (echos) pan from one side to the other adding a lot of motion to the audio part. This is not the same as an auto-pan effect with each delay bouncing hard left/right.

Modulation Delay

Despite its fairly meek exterior, the Modulation Delay is pretty out there. When writing this chapter I was actually tempted to include the Modulation Delay as part of the chorus/ensemble/flanger sections. Why? moddelay

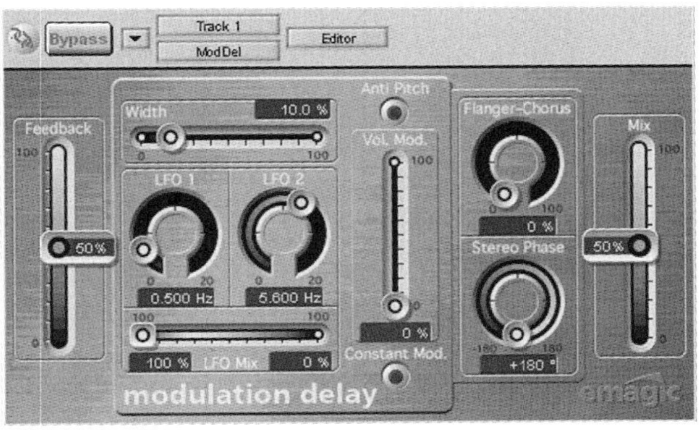

Basically because this fat boy has two (mixable) LFOs, which can be assigned to modulate delay time and amplitude, and because delay times range within a dozen milliseconds.

Due to this special layout, you can actually use the modulation delay as an especially flexible chorus/flanger for those

›robot underwater‹ sounds—great if you're doing a dub for a Thunderbird 4 rescue mission!

For anyone who is wondering about the functionality of the Flanger/Chorus parameter—it does nothing more than control the delay time. If you missed the delay parameter in the Flanger plug-in—the Modulation Delay's the right one for ya!

The inclusion of the Anti-Pitch control avoids wow/flutter distortions which helps keep this bad boy in check.

Sync or Swing

Quite often, you'll want to perfectly synchronize your delays (or LFOs in other FX) so that you have repeats (or phasing/beating/modulations) that are in time with your musical parts ... The bummer is that some of the delay algorithms refer to milliseconds, not to note values and therefore can't be synced to LAM's internal clock without some effort.

To do this, you will need to manually type in a value which matches the song tempo. To work this out, use the following calculation to work out the relationship between Tempo/BPM.

1 second = 1,000 milliseconds (ms)

1 minute = 60 seconds ... so therefore ...

60 (secs) × 1,000 (ms) = 60,000 ms

60,000 divided by BPM = a quarter note (crotchet) value in milliseconds e.g. 60,000/120 BPM = 500 ms

For those of you unfamiliar with note values, here's how to work out what kind of ›note‹ icon to select in the effect interface itself.

Using the calculation above which gives you a quarter note value ... to work out the value of a

- whole note—multiply by the ms value by 4
- half note—multiply by the ms value by 2
- eighth note—divide by the ms value by 2

- sixteenth note—divide by the ms value by 4
- dotted note—multiply by the ms value by 1.5
- triplet note—divide by the ms value by 3

To figure out what the triplet value is of a whole or half note, for example, simply multiply your ms value by the appropriate amount ... and then, with this new value, divide by a third ... it's all pretty simple really!

For the mathematically-challenged among you, I've included a tempo/BPM calculator application which runs under Windows (you'll find it in the shareware folder).

Reverbs

MetalVerbs

If you're using LAM's excellent Platinumverb or Goldverb as the primary reverb on vocals, particularly if you have a long tail (decay) on the sound, you should know that they require far more CPU resources than the Silververb and 3.0 reverb algorithms. It must be said though that the Goldverb is very easy on resources given its quality.

On other material, you may find the less demanding FX are perfectly suited, particularly in the context of the overall mix.

► NB: As the FX quality increases, you will find that the other parameters will have a more subtle effect because the effect's resolution is higher. Solo the track while fine tuning your reverb settings in the Platinumverb.

◎ platinum

Among the key features in the reverbs are the high frequency damping feature, which gives you a more natural, unobtrusive reverberation, and the Room Size and Shape parameters.

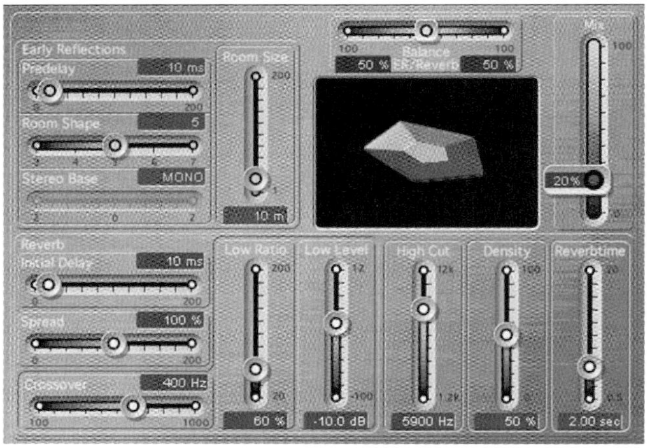

- High frequency Damping does just that—it takes the ›top‹ off the wet signal. In other words, it takes away the brittle and edgy quality of the reverb itself without affecting the original signal. Use it for smooth reverbs.

- For percussion and drums, use smaller rooms with brief delays as they'll sound better. If the delay between dry and wet signals is too great, you'll end up with an indirect sound and dodgy timing.

- The shape of the room (or surfaces in it) can alter the reverb a lot. Imagine a completely cylindrical room. Here there are no flat surfaces for the sound to reflect directly back from, so the reflections tend to ›wash‹ over you. Obviously in the real world, there aren't that many circular rooms, but there are a *lot* of curved surfaces. Keep it in mind.

You should use the Platinum reverb and follow these two basic rules when you're going for natural-sounding rooms:

- In the real world, a large room usually generates a lengthier reverberation.
- The time that elapses prior to the early reflection (Predelay)—in other words, the attack time—has a strong influence on how our ears perceive the size of a room. If you're trying to create the impression of a larger room,

you should give this parameter a nudge. Also adjust the ER/Reverb parameter. This changes the balance between the Early Reflection and the Reverb proper.

- If the Platinum or Goldverb doesn't ›cut it‹ for the final mix and you end up using a third-party reverb, you should still use LAM's internal reverbs while composing and arranging. They'll do just fine as a stand-in for your ›wet dream‹ verb while you're working and allow you more CPU resources to experiment with. The Goldverb uses the same algorithm as the Platinumverb but forgoes the sound-shaping facilities on output which makes it less CPU-hungry. Use it on your busier mixes when computing power is at a premium.

- The other reverbs (Silver and version 3.0) offer less control than the HQ reverbs, but often these will be perfectly usable, even on your final mixdown.

Enverb

enverb

The Enverb— as the name indicates—is a combination of Enveloper and Reverb and is an effect exclusive to Logic Audio users. It allows full envelope control over the shape of the reverbs' diffusion … in other words, you can control the shape of the reverberation (not the original signal … you can use the enveloper for that!) as you would with any synthesizer envelope. This offers ADSR-type controls and visual assistance to aid in the creation of envelope shapes.

Using this facility, combined with the original signal delay parameter you can create gated reverbs, reverse reverbs, pre-reverbs, silly reverbs— and a host of other possibilities.

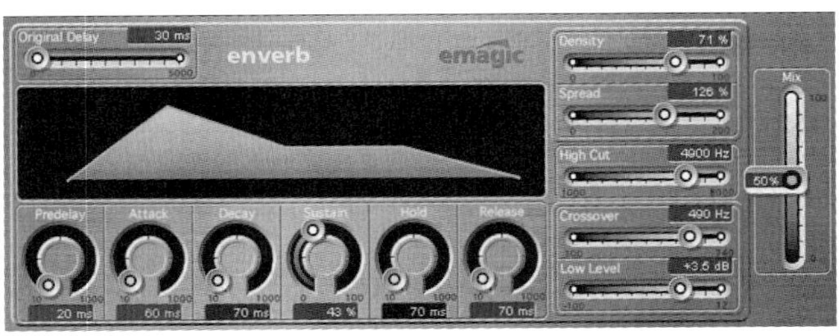

The Enverb's quality is not up to the standard of the Platinum or Gold algorithms but the basic premise behind the effect is as a sound shaping and sculpting tool. If you approach it from this angle you're definitely going to enjoy it.

Bitcrusher

bitsat.wav and bitcrush.wav

The Bitcrusher does nothing more than reduce the signals audio quality on three levels: Clipping, bit resolution and sample rate. Why and when would you want that?

Reducing audio quality is a very useful sound design tool. It makes your signal sound digital, techno, industrial or just weird—depending on the settings and the material. More than useful on drumloops, drums, vocals and bass. Less useful on harmonically rich, chordal stuff.

The bitcrusher does not involve any filtering and therefore sounds purposely cold and digital. Use a DJ EQ inserted after the bitcrusher to smooth out or fatten up the crushed sound.

The graphical display gives you a pretty good picture of what the bitcrusher does to the input signal—its impact is displayed as an abbreviated form of a sine wave. Here's an overview of the parameters and what they're useful for:

- Drive—a digital clipping applied before the bit crushing process. Use it carefully.

- Resolution—setting the bit resolution any lower than 10 bit introduces quantization noise. Check values below 4 for ›radical‹ bit crushing.
- Downsampling—divides the original sample rate by the factor displayed. Since no aliasing filters are involved, you get this special digital pocket calculator feel.
- Clip Level—setting any value below maximum (0.0 db) makes the signal clip at lower levels. The shape of the generated clipping can be switched using the three symbols—with the middle one being the most ›friendly.‹

Pitch Shifter

The Pitch Shifter does just that. It allows you to transpose and or detune an incoming signal. Transposition quality and accuracy gets worse with increased intervals, so be careful when using it on prominent tracks—it won't replace a good background vocal.

pitchshift

The effect has three preset modes allowing for different types of input signals. For anything percussive you should use the ›Drums‹ mode ... and while obvious, the use of this mode on staccato pitched instruments (like clavinets or funk basses) may not be.

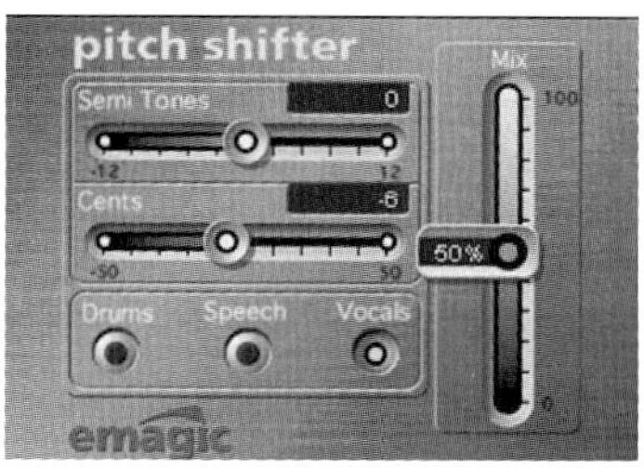

For anything that's pitched and sustained—vocal, guitar, piano parts etc. you should use the Vocal mode.

Detuning the signal by just a few cents creates beating similar to two detuned oscillators in a synthesizer. This fattens up the sound more naturally than a chorus or ensemble effect since no audible modulation is involved. Pitch Shifter is commonly used for doubling vocal tracks, guitar, even strings and other natural sounds.

In comparison to LAM's ›other‹ pitch shifter, the Time and Pitch Machine, the differences are that the TPM is *not* a real-time process and it actually alters your samples.

If you want to generate harmony parts out of existing vocal (or other) audio files, the pitch shifter won't do this for you. That's why the Time and Pitch Machine is there.

If on the other hand, all you want to do is create the impression of a harmony being played or sung ... or you've recorded a vocalist who's take is a little on the ›weak as water‹ side ... try the pitch shifter.

And who knows ... if used with automation, you could do Cher ›Believe‹ covers ... although why you'd want to is a different story.

Dynamic Processors

Compressors

Compression adds ›punch‹ and ›body‹ to your audio. It also keeps errant signal spikes (loud bits) in check and bumps up soft bits by compressing your signal into a defined dynamic range.

LAM 4's compressors all feature an ›autogain‹ function which can be overridden in the higher level versions but which is *always* active in the Silver compressor. This is a ›smart‹ function which ignores your threshold and gain settings to keep normalized levels accurate across the effects input and output. So far, I've found it annoying, particularly when trying to get a really pumpin' drum mix/kick sound etc. For this type of use—dance music guys and gals take note—you should disable this ›feature.‹ If you're new to recording and mixing, then you may be more comfortable leaving it on.

Compression needs to be used as a track insert and is suitable for *all* types of audio. I don't overly recommend using it across an entire mix (as a master insert) because each signal is *very* likely to have different compression needs but see the hints below for some useful settings if you prefer working this way.

compressor

- If you decide to run the whole mix through the compressor—use around a 1.5:1 ratio with fast attack and a medium to slow release time at about –3 dB Threshold.
- For synth strings try 2:1 at –6 dB
- Heavy-handed pianists could do with –6 dB at a 3 or 4:1 ratio
- Acoustic Guitars—try a 2:1 ratio at –7 dB

Threshold settings refer to an input signal peak of 0 dB.

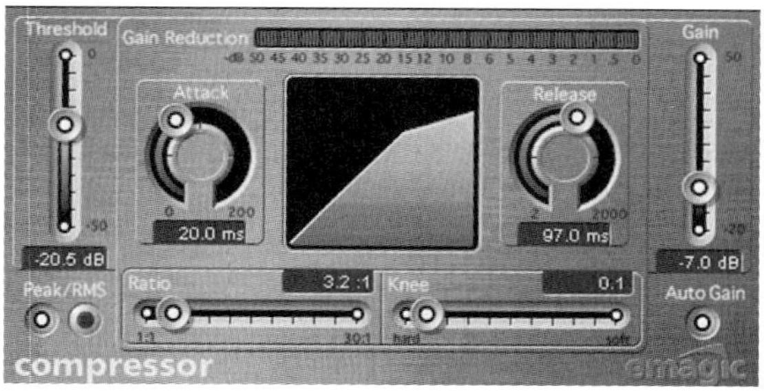

Noise Gate

Gates basically close the volume all the way down whenever the signal level gets below the threshold value. The run-of-the-mill threshold (signal level), attack and release time parameters are there, but a couple of interesting extras make Lam's gate more flexible than other similar Fx you may have tried … namely the …

gater

Hysteresis sets the distance between open and closed threshold—this means: You can not only set the threshold for the gate to close, but also a lower threshold value for it to open again.

With the filters in the sidechain you can limit the frequency range of the signal that triggers the gate. E.g. set the Low Cut control all the way to the right, and a drum loop is gated by its HiHat only.

When setting the filters, check the monitor button to solo the sidechain signal.

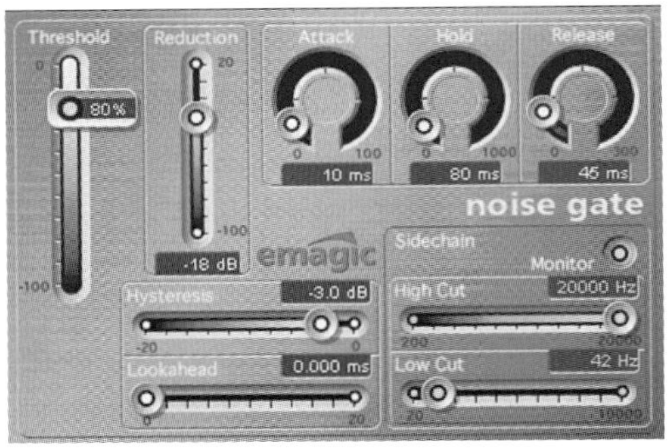

The Lookahead control puts an end to any discussion about the pros and cons of ›analog vs. digital‹ gating—this Noise Gate doesn't create an audible attack slope because it ›knows what's coming‹ before it happens, that's the bottom line.

Expander

expander

An Expander—as the name indicates—is used to expand the dynamics of a signal, i.e. to make loud parts louder and quiet parts quieter.

Its operation is almost identical to that of LAM's compressor/gate.

Where you may find it extremely useful is for bringing overly-compressed takes back to life, for thinning out drumloops, for making the peaks of a percussive track stand out from the rest—you name it.

It is used as an Insert effect.

Spectral Gate

specgate

The Spectral Gate is unique in concept, function—and effort needed to get the hang of it. Just take a look at the LAM manual to see how difficult it is for Emagic themselves to explain!

Here's where you get a behind-the-scenes look at the overall concept and use of this effect.

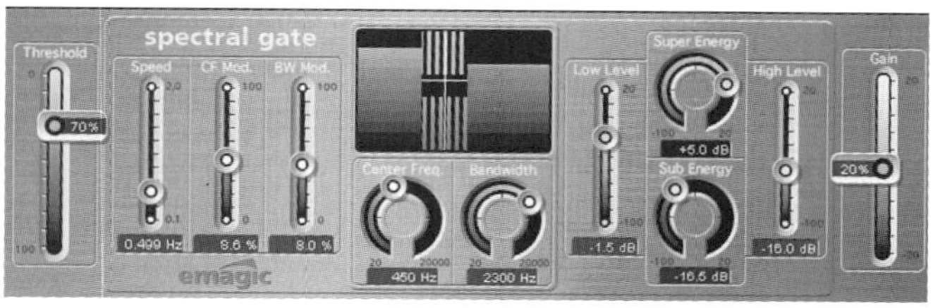

First off, you can define a frequency range by setting the ›Center Frequency‹ and a ›Bandwidth‹ around it. This range is extracted from the input signal using a Fast Fourier Transformation. FFT creates an almost vertical filter slope and is responsible for the stair-like (stepping) artifacts which occur with extreme settings. After setting the frequency range you will notice that frequencies outside this range are muted.

Next step: Set a threshold. The Spectral Gate now ›looks‹ (in real time) at whether the level of the input signal is below or above this threshold.

The parts of the signal that are below the Threshold can now be controlled with the Sub Energy knob, signals above the Threshold are controlled by the Super Energy knob. In this respect the Spectral Gate works like a normal noise gate. But: This all happens within the defined frequency band. Getting an idea of why they called it the Spectral Gate?

The frequency ranges outside the frequency band can be added by the Low Level/High Level sliders, but they are unaffected by the gate.

As if this wasn't enough, the Center Frequency and Bandwidth can also both be modulated by an LFO.

So, now that you know what it does and how it does it, you'd probably like to know what it could possibly be used for, right?

Here are a number of sophisticated applications for drumloops or music passages to give you a bit of a handle on it:

- By setting a high range while passing the rest of the signal through, you can separately control the volume of quiet and loud HiHats—e.g. even them out.
- By setting a narrow bandwidth and modulating the Center frequency with both Sub and Super energy turned all the way down you can create a formant filter effect.
- You can thin out a drumloop, e.g. by completely removing a second, quieter kick drum: All you need to do is: Set a low frequency range, pass the signal above through the Spectral Gate. Now turn Sub energy all the way down and set the Threshold so the quieter kick disappears.
- In reverse, you can easily extract a certain frequency slice from a track while muting the rest. Apply to rhythmic tracks containing drastically varying frequencies to create great rhythmic pads, super submarine kick tracks or really LoFi HiHats.

Since the FFT resolution is limited, the Spectral Gate is very likely to create steps and other artifacts in the signal which adds a lo-fi quality or character. While this may be exactly what you're after, go for EQing, Noise Gates and other tools which don't apply a FFT when you want gentle changes to a ›polite‹ acoustic track.

Enveloper

◎ envelope

LAM's Enveloper lets you shape the attack and release phases of the amplitude (volume) envelope of your audio source. In practice, this will allow you to do obvious things like ›bow‹ a vocal or set up a piano-like attack on a sax sample.

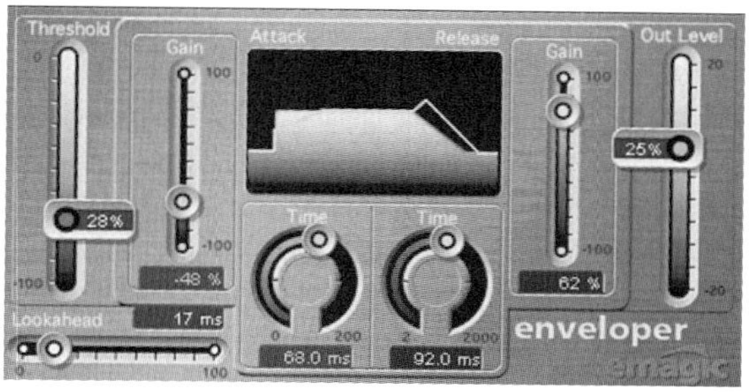

Where I find it particularly cool is to make a part seem slightly off the beat by adding a little bit of attack. Used on the odd track or two—guitar or bass in a soul/funk arrangement as an example—can really make your ›players‹ just enough off the beat to be really ›on.‹ Fans of old James Brown or Barry White tracks will know exactly what this means.

If you're a Robert Fripp fan, then the enveloper is probably gonna appear on 90 % of your guitar tracks—with big attack and release times (and ten other Fx ...). Conversely, you can literally ›percussify‹ (author's license) signals with a soft attack by setting the gain value left of the attack knob to a higher value. Watch the display to monitor how the envelope shape changes with parameter tweaking!

As with many of the other Fx in LAM, this algorithm tracks the incoming audio and retriggers the envelope shape based on variations in amplitude. This is dependent on the threshold and also the amount of ›lookahead‹ time which is set. The shorter the lookahead time, the more pronounced the effect will be.

Use the Enveloper as an Insert on any audio material.

Distortions

LAM 4—like many hardware digital Fx machines—offers two kinds of distortion: Overdrive simulates a Valve Tube Saturation, which sounds warmer and fatter, whereas Distortion creates the character of an overdriven transistor amp—more biting and sharp. This is basically what it's all about when it comes to the ›where to use which?‹ question—use Overdrive to introduce crunch and dirt to sounds like organs, guitars or even drums. Use Distortion for really distorted sounds—metal guitars, techno Fx etc.

◎ distorta and ovadrive

Both, when used in conjunction with other distortions and filters (EQ), can pretty convincingly cover most ›classic‹ guitar amp sounds ranging from ›crunchy‹ Fender amp to ›wall of sound‹ Marshall stack to a punchy Gretsch style simulation …

To set up convincing amp simulations, you must make use of EQs or filters. Pre-shaping the input signal of the distortion effect can prevent harmonics from being distorted. Applying EQing after the distortion allows you to filter unwanted harmonics created by the distortion effect. Both distortion units already have a built-in low pass filter (tone) so post-filtering is not always needed.

Since neither of these effects feature a mix control, you will need to run them as Send effects in order to combine distorted and clean signals—common e.g. with ›grunge‹

tracks. Try pre-fader mode for controlling the volume of the clean signal independently.

Optimizing Effects Levels

When using effects plug-ins, as with all of your audio routing, it's essential that you set up the best possible signal level. Dependent on whether you're using the busses or insert Fx, the following section will cover some basic tips for optimizing levels to ensure that you get the best results.

Adjusting the Effects Input

You can change the output level of an effect by reducing the level of the signal that you're routing to its input. There are a few exceptions to this rule such as special plug-ins (third-party) that generate signals internally, but they are rare.

When you're routing signals via Send, use the Send knob to set the input level for the individual busses. Don't forget Pre and Post fader modes either, but remember that this will affect the tonality as a totally different signal may be being routed to the bus input.

Additionally, you should ensure that the bus input (channel Send knob) and output (bus fader) signals are balanced properly so that you don't encounter undesirable side-effects like:

- Digital distortion within the plug-in caused by overloading the input as the bus output level is too high.
- Dynamic processors don't work properly because plug's input level does not match the threshold.
- The effect output is too high and overdrives subsequent plugs or the channel's output—particularly problematic with distortions. Use the output gain control to adjust the output level of the plug-in.

When using an Insert effect, the Mix or Gain parameter is the only tool that you have at your disposal for changing the relationship between the wet and dry signals. This may be different with third-party plug-ins.

Mono or Stereo Plug-ins—Avoiding Problems

As mentioned earlier, LAM 4 will automatically select plug-ins appropriate to the audio object's I/O flow, but it is possible to override these settings by pressing and holding [alt] before selecting the plug-in flip menu on an audio object.

Every plug-in type (mono/mono, mono/stereo or stereo/stereo) can—theoretically—be used regardless on both mono and stereo audio tracks ... *but* ...

- If you place a stereo in/out effect in a mono audio signal channel, then you won't be able to fully exploit the spatial advantages of the plug-in because you can only use the left side of the effect.
- Similarly, a mono effect used on a stereo channel will ruin your stereo image.
- *All* plug-ins which do *not* match the currently selected audio object's signal I/O flow will require a data stream conversion. A conversion requires some additional CPU load, so therefore it's a better idea to choose a plug-in which matches the signal, i.e. mono input for a mono track, stereo input for a stereo track.
- All plug-ins marked with an asterisk *(s/s) require a data stream conversion, so the tip above applies here.
- Stereo/stereo effects use more processing power than the other effect types, so if you have a stereo signal which doesn't absolutely, positively, need to be processed in stereo, use the mono/stereo alternative. Needless to say, this is only if your computer is choking on the workload and does *not* apply to insert effects.
- Mono/stereo Fx are great if you want to make a mono source sound ›wider‹ or ›deeper.‹
- Some third-party Fx have internal input/output level controls which can affect the overall volume of the signal

being routed thru them. If something is suddenly distorting, check to see if this is the culprit.

- Some third-party stereo plug-ins feature separate meters and controls for each side of the effect.
- If you decide to use a plug-in with a mono input (m/s) on a stereo channel, then only the left channel of the direct signal is processed by the effect, the right channel essentially bypasses the effect. At the same time, the output signal of the plug-in consists of an equal measure of both sides of the stereo channel—i. e. 50:50 of wet and dry on both sides.

Plug-in Economy

Generally—especially if you're new to LAM—it's a good idea to monitor CPU load while setting up plug-ins and EQS.

During the creation of a song or while just messing around you may temporarily need to use more plugs than actually required by your final mix. Sometimes, it's a case of ›just *this* one plug too many‹ that makes your CPU choke or negatively affects the overall performance. To reduce the plug-in load temporarily there's a couple of options:

The System performance window from the Audio menu displays CPU load and drive performance in real time.

- Plug-ins only use CPU power when activated. Click the Bypass button of a plug that's not currently in use, and the CPU resources will be released.
- Setting the Mix fader to 0 % does not have any influence on CPU consumption.
- If you're sure you won't require the further use of a plug, remove it. Active plug-ins suck CPU power even if they are used on muted tracks or if they are not routed to any audible output.
- Use platinum or full stereo versions economically. A pad that runs in the background does not need a platinum reverb.

- When using one effect for numerous tracks make use of busses (see ›Fx Routing and Mixing‹ from page 107 onwards). Each instance of a plug-in uses extra CPU power.
- Of course this only applies to send effects like reverbs or chorus effects, whereas insert effects are exclusive to a track.
- As a rule of thumb: Set up two or three general reverbs on separate busses rather than activating an individual reverb plug for each track. Apart from reducing CPU load, this keeps your mix clean and easier to handle. It might be a good idea to set up a general, simple reverb for your autoload song so you can instantly add ambience to a new track. This saves time and allows at least a ›taste test‹ of the enhancement on your monitor mix. You can obviously replace this reverb with a much better one when doing your fix on the (final) mix.
- When constructing a track, check the mixer page regularly for superfluous plug-ins. Also check for where a platinum version or a Fat EQ could be replaced by a less power consuming alternative without affecting the overall mix.
- Try to set up the basic arrangement for a song without any plug-ins. Resist the—pretty understandable—temptation to make each track perfect right after recording. Wait for compression or EQing at least until you have set up the basic arrangement. Needless to say, this speeds up song creation big time.

11 Track Bouncing

Over the preceding chapters, you've probably noticed references to ›bouncing‹ of tracks. Here's where I make good on my promise and spill the beans.

For you younger readers, ›bouncing‹ is a term that dates back to the days when 4-track tape recorders were considered ›state of the art‹ equipment. This process allowed you to record the output of one or more tracks, and an external signal if you wished, to another tape track to free tracks—because the track number was very limited, obviously.

The downside with bouncing on analog tape is that with each successive bounce (or pass), a little bit of extra tape noise is added to your recording and the overall audio quality is reduced.

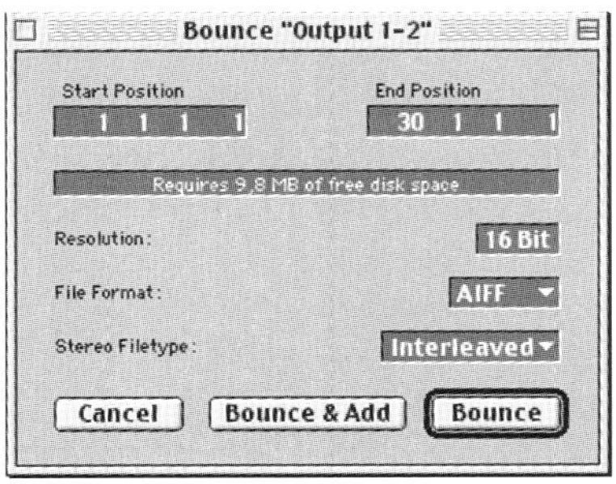

LAM's Bounce window accessed via the bounce (BNCE) button on the master fader.

Nowadays, with digital recording systems like LAM, the noise limitation and audio quality reduction isn't too much of a problem so virtually infinite bouncing is possible. The reason why?

Digital systems don't add audible noise because the combining of tracks is simply a merging of data which represents your audio. As this is a collection of numbers, not magnetic particles on tape there is no physical reason why the signal quality should degrade.

There is, however, the issue of ›dithering‹ which can affect the quality of digital bouncing. Bouncing is almost always a compromise—it can reduce the bit resolution of the signal, which is especially problematic with low level passages, and, obviously, following bouncing you can no longer mix or process tracks independently within the bounced file.

Conservation Issues

One major plus with LAM's bounce facility is its ability to free up system resources—in both the number of tracks and effects—available for use in your overall mix.

At this stage, you should have a pretty good handle on the CPU power needed by LAM's internal and third-party FX.

I'd be willing to wager that even if you do have a superfast G3 with loads of RAM, mag wheels and racing stripes—one day (soon) you will run out of CPU resources when doing a mixdown. This is where bouncing comes to the rescue by allowing you to record a new audio file i. e. your original signal(s) *plus* effects/EQs etc. (or multiple tracks without FX).

► Once this is done, you can simply use the new audio file(s) ›dry,‹ mute the old ones and bypass or delete their plug-in assignments. Make sure to always save an old version of your arrangement. This gives you the option to correct things should you find yourself with a bounce result that's less than perfect.

To bounce a track (or multiple tracks) in LAM, use the following steps.

1. Set up whatever effects and levels/automation info etc. you want to use in the mixer and route the audio tracks you want to bounce to a specific bus or output.
2. Mute everything you *don't* wish to bounce.

3 *If* you're using busses, ensure that the bus output is set to an appropriate Master output.

4 Scroll to the appropriate Master fader (Output 1-2, 3-4 etc.).

5 Click on the BNCE button to open the Bounce window.

6 Select the start and end positions. If there are previously selected audio regions in the Arrange window, the bounce locators are automatically set to match this range. In Version 4 there are also a couple of further options described below.

7 Press bounce and when prompted, type in a file name and set a folder for the resulting file. When done, click Save.

8 This will generate a new audio file and is a real-time process.

Bit Resolution

New to version 4 is the option to select a different bit resolution when bouncing. Needless to say, this is dependent on your audio hardware, so *don't* select 24 bit if your card isn't able to record/playback at 24-bit res. It will *not* make it sound better, but it *will* increase the size of the file significantly. Use this option only if the resulting file will be used in a 24-bit system.

Another point is that the bit resolution selected should be appropriate to the project. If you want to bounce to an 8-bit file for Internet delivery then use it, if you're doing a CD, you should stick to 16 bit. This is obvious, I know, but the temptation to use 24 bit ›because it's gotta be better‹ ain't necessarily always the case.

- 8 bit—this is the option you should choose if you're doing a multimedia CD-ROM or intend on using your bounced file on the Internet. 8-bit files are far smaller than their 16-bit counterparts and sacrifice audio quality as the trade-off for this reduced size. In return: Never use 8 bit in the middle of arranging just in order to save hard disk space—you won't be able to restore the original audio quality from an 8-bit file.
- 16 bit—this is likely to be the resolution of choice for most people and is the rate used on CDs, which is presumably

where your music is gonna end up. If your final product is going to be an audio CD, use (the default choices of) 16 bit, 44.1 kHz stereo interleaved when bouncing.

- 24 bit—this is the ›next generation‹ of hardware's bit resolution and is the resolution used by DVD-ROM for audio storage. As I've mentioned elsewhere in the book, there are a limited number of devices which support this resolution. If you have the hardware capable of 24 bit/96 kHz and are doing a DVD, then by all means, use these higher end options.

Sample Rate

Although sample rate is not an option in the Bounce window, it is *very* relevant to the format of your final bounced file.

Again, like bit resolution, only a few devices support 96-kHz sample rate. LAM's sample rate is set globally in the Audio menu—options depend on the hardware used.

If the hardware is flexible enough, it is selectable between 44.1 kHz and 96 kHz with other sample rates available (48 and 88.2 kHz).

If you want to generate files using a sample rate lower than 44.1 kHz, then you will probably need to use a third-party application to convert the bounced file afterwards (see Peak on the CD-ROM).

- 44.1 kHz—used for CD and given that any bounced ›master‹ files that you generate require no further conversion (which will affect the signal quality), you can directly ›burn‹ these to an audio CD.
- 48 kHz—most often used for video post-production work and for printing to DAT.
- 88.2 kHz—unusual sample rate with applications limited to a small percentage of post-production and DVD work.
- 96 kHz—this is the ›next generation‹ sample rate (combined with 24-bit resolution) which is used in a handful of

high-end DAW's like Pro Tools and is the format for DVD audio.

Interleaved or Split Stereo

You can generate a pair of mono files or a single stereo file.

- Stereo Interleaved is a single stereo file. It is the choice for most applications—e.g. for further use in LAM as well as for mastering.
- Split Stereo is a combination of two separate mono (L and R) files. The respective right and left channels are saved as individual mono SDII/WAV OR AIFF files. LAM conveniently attaches an L or R to the file name to identify the channel. You should only use this format if you want to use an audio editor or CD-writing app that can only deal with mono audio. Another use for Split Stereo is on signals that you want to edit separately, i.e. when you're dealing with L and R sides of a sample that contain different material.

► While bouncing always watch the peak indicator in the master channel. If it's lit after the bounce, reduce your Bus or Master levels and re-do the bounce.

► When setting the range for the bounce, make sure to leave space for reverb decays or a delay fading out.

Bouncing the Effect Output

If you see the dreaded ›Pad Overload‹ message when you've gone overboard with Fx and EQ plug-ins but still have a few audio tracks available, you can use them to record pure effects signals—i. e. no dry signal, just pure and wet. This trick is best suited to effects like reverb or delay and, depending on the situation, you can record a discrete effects file for each original signal or one effect file for use with several original signals (e. g. a reverb only file). The best method is to pull the faders for the dry signals all the way down and limit control of the effect to the Pre-Fader Send knob. This way, you can record just the ›wet‹ signal by bouncing the track.

One of the cool things about recording an effects signal in this way is that you can do all kinds of stuff with the signal—now an audio file—that you couldn't if it were just the output signal of an effects plug-in. These include all of the Digital Factory and Sample Editor functions for effects like gating, chopping, inserting silence, fading in and out, reversing the sample etc. etc.

Oh ... nearly forgot to mention that there's nothing to stop you from routing this audio file through another effect and bouncing that as well. In the words of the immensely talented (yes Virginia, that *is* sarcasm) Two Unlimited ›there's no limit.‹

Creating Reversed Effects

Bouncing also offers creative options, such as the following.

1. Record an audio file and do any ›top and tailing‹ (cutting of dead space at the beginning and end of the file) that's necessary.
2. Reverse the audio file by opening it in the Sample Editor and selecting ›Reverse‹ from the Options menu. Ensure that you make a backup when prompted as a precaution.
3. Run the audio file through an effect—e.g. reverb and customize to taste.
4. Bounce the reversed and effected audio file, ensuring that you leave a bar or so at the end to capture any decay of the effect that may be present.
5. Open the new bounced audio file in the Sample Editor and reverse it again.
6. Save the file.

There you have it! An audio file complete with a funky reversed reverb effect on it ... and it's oh so seventies and eighties, retro fans.

There's nothing to stop you from using bounce again on the same audio file to add different combinations of forward/ backwards effects—and remember, you can select just a portion of the audio file that you want to mess with (before or after the bounce—or both!), not to mention pure effects only signals. Starting to see some interesting possibilities?

Creating Final Mixes Using Bounce

You can use bouncing to combine *all* of your tracks into a stereo AIFF file for direct burning to a CD or printing to DAT. Here's how you create your final mix using the bounce function:

1. Since the Bounce function ignores everything but audio files, you need to record your MIDI sound sources as audio signals, dedicating a mono or stereo audio track to each MIDI sound (if possible) which allows you a range of further FX processing options.
2. If you're running out of audio tracks (or your computer is choking on the workload), set up any necessary MIDI mix automation and/or levels and record all MIDI signals to one stereo audio track. Record important tracks like bass or lead separately though.
3. If your computer is already maxed out, you can alternatively do a bounce of your audio parts. Next, copy the resulting bounced audio file back into the Arrange window. Mute the other audio tracks (or pack them into a folder and mute it) and then record your MIDI tracks as audio.
4. Use track bouncing to generate a Stereo Interleaved file. Make sure to leave a pre- and post-roll when setting the range in the Bounce window.
5. Now for some finishing touches: Import the master file that you just generated to a new song and open it in the sample editor.
6. Select the entire file via ⌘A and Normalize it to bring the file up to maximum level.
7. Still in the Sample Editor, select the intro preceding the first signal (by clicking and dragging the mouse so that the section you want to silence is highlighted) and apply Silence (found in the Functions menu) to erase any noise that may be on this portion of the audio file.

Mastering tip: Most consumer CD players don't track all that accurately. Ensure that you leave 100 to 150 milliseconds as an intro and outro to your songs, to avoid CD players ›skipping‹ over your masterpiece(s).

Follow the same procedure for the outro at the end of the track. If you like, you can use Fade In/Out Before Inserting Silence.

8 Select the entire file using ⌘A and Save Selection As from the File menu. Save and name the selected audio region as a new file and, when prompted, leave the default 1,000 ms top/tail.

Tip: Don't forget that normalizing can introduce quantize noise, so make sure you have a backup copy of the entire file to fall back on.

The result is a normalized, final cut of a CD audio master file in AIFF Stereo Interleaved format. With a CD-R recorder and the requisite software (Adaptec Toast for example), you can burn the song directly onto an audio CD.

Mastering: Avoiding Problems

Although track bouncing is fairly straightforward you should, at least consider, the following issues.

So, You Wanna Make a CD

If you eventually want to commit your masterpieces to CD (don't we all?), you should work (and this means recording too) in the recommended audio format in LAM from the start: 16 bit and 44.1 kHz, even if your hardware is capable of higher rates/bit resolutions ... as I mentioned earlier.

This not only saves time and effort, but any ›morning after‹ format conversion for audio export can lead to round-off error and digital filtering, which translates into signal degradation. Converting a 44.1 kHz recording upwards to 48, 88 or 96 kHz makes no sense whatsoever, as roundoff error will make your audio sound crappy. These higher rates are of no use for CD either.

Reverb and Delay Tails

When adding reverb or delay effects, ensure you adjust the right Locator *before* you bounce so that the decay phase of the effects signal is not cut off. It's always preferable to leave too much space rather than too little.

Peripheral Noise

Obviously, you should mute all audio tracks that you don't need before you bounce the tracks that you do need.

If you have enough CPU resources, you can save the time and effort of setting up mix automation by using a noise gate as the last insert of each channel that needs to be automated.

Less obviously, muting is also necessary for all of the effects that you don't need. Active send effects can add background noise even when they aren't receiving input signals.

To do this, use automation on the bypass or on/off parameter of LAM's internal effects and third party plugs if available.

These mute/unmutes can be recorded in real time on a track by track basis, by use of the technique described in ›Snapshot Automation‹ on page 116 or inserted as events on a newly-created Audio Mix (A-Playback) sequence via the Event List editor.

Backups

Before using track bouncing to combine tracks or go nuts with effects, you should make a backup copy of your original audio file(s). Backup copies give you a ›fall back‹ position should things screw up and allow you the freedom to experiment with different settings for bouncing (or indeed any type of mixdown).

12 Mixing-Tricks

This chapter takes a look at some general mixdown tips, tricks, do's and don'ts that apply to any mixing situation, not just to LAM.

The ›Because I Can‹ Syndrome

So, you've got yourself a G6/1000, with a Zybox cryogenic cooling system and ten terabytes of RAM so you can put EQs and multiple insert Fx on every channel *and* play Quake II at the same time!—Good for you!

Now to get a little realistic about this, you should avoid the use of dozens of EQs and Fx on every track, just because you can. Rather, you should concentrate on getting your recordings right in the first place, so all of that other bullshit isn't necessary.

I can't remember which famous composer said it, but to paraphrase ›music is the space between the notes.‹ With this in mind, chant the mantra ›less is more‹ every time you find that you've been ›tweaking‹ a sound's EQ or Fx settings for more than a minute or two. If you're screwing around this much, it probably means the sound is wrong for the track.

No-one Knows Everything

Recognize that even the most experienced engineers and the most famous musicians once weren't that way. Secondly, recognize that these people would be the first to ask for help if they needed it—that's how they got so smart and/or famous. So, ask ›dumb‹ questions on the Users group, at your local music store, talk with your friends and bounce ideas off each other. Knowledge is one thing where too much is never enough. So, put your pride and ego on the shelf.

The Sum of the Parts

Any final mix is made up of a number of individual parts. Pretty obvious, I know, but a lot of people forget that the ›individual‹ parts should be just that—individual.

What I mean by this, is that quite often when arranging, many musicians will simply use something because ›it sounds good.‹ The problem is that the part may not make musical sense when listened to in isolation or, as your arrangement grows, that ›because it sounds good‹ part becomes superfluous. In general, if every musical part makes ›sense‹ on its own then your overall arrangement will benefit.

The individual parts should have their own ›breathing space‹ which can certainly be achieved with EQs and Fx to make them stand out, *but* you may find that taking a different approach to your *arrangement* delivers a stronger result.

To this end, I encourage you to try a counter-melody variation, a sustained rather than moving string section or my personal fave—delete or mute parts—to bring your individual tracks out of the mix before resorting to EQs and/or Fx to ›fix‹ things.

Light and Shade

Although a busy arrangement is impressive, it becomes dull after 30 seconds or so, dependent on your individual attention span. Drop parts out, bring them back in, change melody line instrument sounds, double bass parts to add drive (›oomph!!!‹) to your music.

Listen to Mozart or Prince and you'll hear how the use of ›busy‹ and then quiet passages adds incredible impact to your music. You'll probably find that the individual instrument lines will remain in your memory as separate entities as well as being part of the overall orchestration.

Each part makes an impact when everything (or almost everything) else drops out and the full-blown orchestration makes an impact because of its volume and dynamics when compared to the solo (or quieter) part.

About Effects

Add effects (reverb, chorus, delay etc.) *after* you have experimented with at least a ›shell‹ arrangement. This allows you more ›space‹ to add (or delete) countermelodies or rhythms which may benefit your music.

Too much reverb/chorus etc. may make your piece sound ›muddy‹ as the coloration added by the effect may increase some overtones of particular sounds, causing them to overlap and thereby reduce the impact of the instruments' individuality.

Use of effects should be judicious. If your song doesn't need them for the entire track, then don't use them, except where required. This will assist in the light/shade of your music and will add even more impact when coupled with the previously discussed dropping in and out of tracks.

NB: When switching effects on and off, be careful where you place them in your track as this may take a second or two to ›kick in‹ (i.e. to start effecting the sound).

If your computer can handle it—and if it can't reread the Bouncing chapter—you should only use the hi-quality versions of the effects, rather than compromising so you can do the mix in one pass. The lo-fi Fx alternatives will be just that—lo-fi—and so will your final mix.

Frequency Issues

Carefully select the instruments/samples you want to use in your piece. When orchestrating, take into account the various frequencies that each instrument or sample occupies.

(Remember that stuff we looked at in the EQ/FX chapter?) There's no point in picking a bunch of samples (or MIDI-based instruments) which all fall into the same range because you'll spend days EQing trying to make them all work together—and you'll probably end up picking different samples, changing sounds, swearing a lot and kicking the family pet.

Save yourself the time and effort (and save your pet the pain and confusion).

Cymbals, hi-hats, cowbells etc. as instruments, cannot be varied in pitch, but they do contain a lot of shared high frequency harmonics. Bass guitars and kick drums also suffer from similar shared frequencies or bandwidths at the other end of the audio spectrum. You should aim for a balanced mix which allows space for each instrument to be heard clearly within the context of the entire arrangement.

Pan

Setting up different ›fixed‹ pan positions for individual sounds within the mix assists in separating tracks/frequencies. Avoid extreme and therefore unnatural settings though, rather use 80 % left or right.

Automated panning is very effective for adding animation to your music. However, overuse can confuse the listener.

The best instruments to autopan are short percussive ones—e. g. sequenced parts, clav etc. or alternately a horn or string wash which pans—slowly—from one side to the other while sustaining.

Environmental Audio

Try to listen to your final mixes through as many different types of amp/speaker combos as possible. If you have a CD-burner, run off a copy and listen to your track(s) on the hi-fi in the lounge room, your boom-box or car stereo. You'd be amazed at how shitty your ›magic, best I've ever done‹ mix can sound through other systems.

You'll probably make a few ›coasters‹ with your blank CDs, but persevere until you find that balance where your mixes sound good (or at least passable) on everything you play them on. Realistically, this sort of second-rate audio equipment is what 99 % of your potential audience will actually be listening to your music on.

Over the next couple of chapters you'll find a glossary of terms and info on a whole lotta resources for you to check out, both online and on the CD.

Appendix

Wizoo Online Support

Updated Book Info

A Web page is dedicated to each book in the Wizoo series. Feel free to check it out for the latest news on the book, new system versions, links to hip Web sites, pages with patches and info.

Punch the following address into your browser:

`http://www.wizoo.com/docs/english/bookservice/lam.htm`

Exploit this information and these resources—you'll save time, meet other like-minded folks and possibly learn a thing or two.

Web Site

If you run into problems that this book can't help you with, Wizoo offers comprehensive online support on a wide range of topics in the field of electronic sound generation, synthesizers and Midi. When you're in a major hurry to solve a problem, go directly to the ›Content‹ area of our site:

`http://www.wizoo.com/`

- Take a look at our FAQs—here you'll find answers to frequently asked questions on a wide variety of subjects.
- Our link pages containing more than 600 music links will help you find other Internet sites that deal your topics of interest.
- You'll find basic information on, and a general introduction to, digital audio and related topics in our Newbie Section.
- You can also search our Web site for a specific term: Simply click on ›Search‹ located on the navigation frame to go to the Search page.

Email

If neither the book (and accompanying CD-ROM) nor the Web site can help you find a solution to the problem you're confronted with, feel free to use our free-of-charge troubleshooting hotline. Email your question to:

Address: `userinput@wizoo.com`
Subject: `LAM <Brief description of the problem>`
(e. g. `>Your tip doesn't work in my setup<`)

Anyone who owns a WIZOO LAM guide is welcome to use this service—we do however ask that you do us a favor and stick to these basic prerequisites:

- One book-related question per email only.
- Keep your email short and to the point.
- Please be patient with us, our crew handles up to several hundred questions on peak days.
- Bear with us, we're unable to guarantee a comprehensive solution to every problem. With a program as complex as LAM, there is always a potential for problems that can't be solved from afar and/or are due to your setup's configuration; in these cases, we'll forward your email to the manufacturer's hotline.

Try to keep these items in mind when dropping us a line, and we should be able to help you out. Not much to ask in return for a free-of-charge service, is it?

CD-ROM

You'll find Q and A's (in hypertext format) as well as Internet support links on the accompanying CD-ROM.

These cover a number of commonly asked questions and a few of the more esoteric or obscure ones as well.

If you have a problem which isn't addressed within this documentation or in the guide, please let us know via the email address above and we'll do our best to answer your question(s) ASAP.

Before you do this, however, take a look at the bookservice page or my FAQ site—`http://www.ozemail.com.au/~oscwilde/index.html`

LAM Internet Links

Check out the Book Support page at the WIZOO Website. This support page features a regularly updated list of LAM Links.

`http://www.wizoo.com/docs/english/bookservice/lam.htm`

Below are a bunch of links to Web sites that provide information, updates, contacts and FAQs on LAM and related topics. These are also available on the CD as HTML.

Emagic Germany: `http://www.emagic.de/`

Emagic's own pages featuring FAQs, Q & A's, updates and other downloads.

Logic Users Mailing List: `http://www.mcc.ac.uk/~emagic/`

Here you can subscribe to the Logic Users mailing list and talk to like-minded folks every day for the rest of your life.

My LAM FAQ Pages:
`http://www.ozemail.com.au/~oscwilde/index.html`

Surprisingly, FAQs on LAM are answered here. You'll find the info from the CD plus a heap of other updated stuff here.

Plug-ins Available for LAM

To add to the versatility of LAM, third-party effects plug-ins are available for download and purchase at most of the following URLs. You'll find a number of demo versions to test-drive on the accompanying CD-ROM, saving you the download time and cost of Internet access. Also featured is support documentation and purchasing details for many of these software marvels. To ensure that you invest in the right plug-ins, we recommend that you check out our ›Wizoo Guide VST Plug-ins.‹

Arboretum Systems: `http://www.arboretum.com/`
Hyperprism—excellent and flexible collection of over twenty effects and Raygun noise removal software, plus other cool tools.

TC Works: `http://www.tcworks.de/`
Truly awesome Reverb, EQ and more. Division of TC Electronic, makers of high-end (and I mean high-end) professional studio FX.

Waves: `http://www.waves.com/`
Outstanding Native Power Pack with True Verb, C1 Compressor/Gate, Q10 ParaGraphic EQ, L1 Ultra Maximizer, S1 Stereo Imager and more.

Glossary

Active MIDI Transmission (AMT)—Emagic devised combination of hardware and software that provides tighter MIDI timing through a sophisticated buffering scheme. Currently, only the AMT8 and Unitor8 interfaces from Emagic support it.

AD converters (ADC)—Short for ›analog/digital;‹ a device that converts (via sampling) an analog signal to a digital signal that represents equivalent information.

ADAT—Digital 8-track audio recorder by Alesis based on video tape; the standard device in its class; diverse generations and models are available.

ADAT Optical—Optical interface for parallel transmission of eight audio channels via fiber-optic cable. Now the established standard for digital multi-channel interfaces.

ADSR—Short for ›Attack, Decay, Sustain, Release‹—These four phases are found on synthesizer envelopes and in some of the LAM effects. ⇨Envelope.

AES/EBU—Short for ›Audio Engineering Society/European Broadcast Union;‹ this is the association's standard transmission format for professional stereo digital audio signals

AIFF—Digital audio format used on Macintosh computers

Aliasing—Digital artifact which is caused by trying to digitally record signals that contain frequencies above half the sample rate.

Amplitude—term used to describe the amount of a signal. It can relate to volume in an audio signal or the amount of voltage in an electrical signal. In the audio sector, the term is often equated with ›level‹ and ›volume.‹

AMT—Short for ⇨›Active MIDI Transmission‹

API—abbrev. of Application Programming Interface. Steinberg's VST is an API which Emagic used to interface with LAM, allowing access to ⇨VST plug-ins.

Attack—Start phase of a sonic event

ASIO—Short for ›Audio Stream Input Output;‹ a Steinberg designed ⇨API which is used to create software drivers for the communication between audio hardware and audio application (e.g. LAM).

Audio file—A file that actually contains digital audio data, as opposed to ⇨audio regions or audio segments.

Audio region—This simulated audio file holds the place for an actual ⇨audio file or portions thereof; it doesn't contain audio data, only peripheral information such as the start and end point.

Audio segment—Same as ⇨audio region

Audiosuite—Plug-in effect format. Non-realtime and destructive in LAM's Sample Edit window.

Aux—Short for auxiliary; in mixers, these circuits are usually identical to effects sends.

Boost—General term for amplifying or increasing the level of signals.

Bpm—Short for ›Beats Per Minute‹ increments of musical tempo (1 beat = 1 quarter note).

Bus—In computer jargon, this general term refers to data, address and control circuits. The ⇨Cpu communicates with peripheral devices and expansion cards via a bus (⇨Pci, ⇨Scsi).

Bus width—Refers to the maximum number of bits that can be transported via the ⇨Bus simultaneously.

Busmaster cards—Internal computer expansion cards that access the system memory to execute data transport without requiring ⇨Cpu performance and thus free performance power for other tasks.

Cache—a type of high-speed ⇨Ram found on computer mainboards or inside Cpus. It is used as temporary memory by the processor to execute software instructions more quickly than with the main system Ram.

Cd audio—Short for ›Compact Disc—Audio;‹ current standard for stereo music Cds: 44.1 kHz ⇨sample rate and 16-bit word width.

Cd-R—Short for ›Cd-Recordable;‹ The term describes a blank Cd. It is placed in a ⇨Cd-R recorder to burn digital data onto the Cd (cannot be deleted/overwritten).

Cd-R recorder—Also called ›Cd burner‹ or ›toaster;‹ device used to burn data onto Cd-Rs, can also usually be used as a Cd-Rom drive.

Cd-ripper—A software program that reads audio Cds and converts the data into ⇨Wav/⇨Aif file format for use with digital audio applications, like Lam. This process is entirely digital and results in no loss of audio quality.

Cd-Rw—Short for ›Cd-ReWritable;‹ (a.k.a. Cde—Compact Disc Eraseable) Similar to ⇨Cd-R, although here data can be deleted and overwritten.

Clipping—An artifact introduced when an audio signal is recorded at too high a level—the loudest parts of the signal are cut off or clipped.

Clock—Frequency specification (usually in MHz) that describes how fast the computer can execute certain operations. The specification for processors is the most widely-known clock type; it pertains to the computing cycle of the CPU. Bus clock is also crucial to performance; it describes at which rate the CPU can communicate with other computer components via the busses.

Comb Filtering—Filter curve with steep notches, which in a graphical representation, resemble the teeth of a comb. Changes the timbre of a sound drastically and is usually considered an undesirable side effect caused by phase shifting, among others.

CPU—Short for ›Central Processing Unit;‹ the main processor of a computer system.

Crossfade—A crossfade is where one audio region is reduced in volume as another audio region is increased in volume thereby fading into one another.

DA converter (DAC)—Short for ›digital/analog converter;‹ a device that changes an analog signal into a digital signal that represents equivalent information via ⇨sampling.

DAW—Short for ›digital audio workstation;‹ a device that is used for the recording, mixing, effecting and playback of digital audio. These usually feature dedicated hardware components in conjunction with a computer running dedicated software.

dB—Short for ›decibel;‹ a numerical expression for the relative (a logarithmic value) loudness of a sound. Different measures of dB such as dB u or dB V are used depending on the application and nominal value.

Destructive—›Destructive audio processing‹ means that the actual audio data in an ⇨audio file is changed as opposed to just editing peripheral or playback parameters.

DIMM—Short for ›Dual In-line Memory Module;‹ board equipped with ⇨RAM memory components; it is plugged into appropriate ⇨slots on the mainboard.

Disk At Once—⇨CD-R recorder mode: All tracks are written to the ⇨CD-R without interruption. This mode is generally required to write on CDs in ⇨CD audio format. Not all CD-R recorders can operate in this mode (⇨Track At Once).

Drivers—Files (usually system extensions) required by the Mac OS so that it can address expansion components such as hard disks, MIDI interfaces or soundcards.

DSP—Short for ›Digital Signal Processor,‹ a computer chip designed specifically for computing audio data. This type of chip is installed in some audio cards for computing effects and related data without the help of the CPU.

Duplex—parallel operation of audio inputs and outputs of ⇨soundcards. Half-duplex means that an audio card does not support simultaneous recording and playback operation. Full-duplex means that you can use inputs and outputs simultaneously.

DVD—Short for ›Digital Versatile Disk,‹ a format that is the designated successor to contemporary CDs (⇨CD audio). These disks hold video and audio data. With massive storage capacity of seventeen gigabyte (equivalent to 25 conventional CDs); the format for audio DVD is 24 bit/96 kHz.

EASI—Short for ›Enhanced Audio Streaming Interface;‹ an Emagic designed ⇨API which is used to create software drivers for the purpose of getting audio into and out of a computer via a soundcard.

E-IDE—Short for ›Enhanced ⇨IDE;‹ which is exactly what it actually is. Nowadays, most people refer to Ultra-ATA and/or E-IDE hard disks simply as IDE.

Envelope—Envelopes are found in synthesizers and some of LAM's effects. They are used to control volume and other levels (tonal color, for example) of a sound over time.

FIFO—Short for ›First In First Out,‹ which determines how data is transported into and out of a buffer. Kind of a first come, first served line.

FPU—Short for ›Floating Point Unit;‹ a computer component, subroutine or algorithm that executes floating point calculations. These operations are crucial in realtime audio computing.

Full-duplex—⇨Duplex.

Gain—In audio jargon, this term is equivalent to level. For filters, it describes the degree of boost/cut in ⇨dB.

Graphics Card—A Computer card that is physically inserted in a Pci slot in modern Macintoshs. Its function is to display images and text on a computer monitor (screen). Some Macintoshs have a graphics chipset and video memory which is mounted on the mainboard which does the same job.

Half-duplex—⇨Duplex.

I/O—Short for ›Input/Output.‹

Ide—Short for ›Integrated Device (or Drive, depending on who you ask) Electronics,‹ a ⇨Bus used to connect compatible devices such as or Cd-Rom or hard drives.

Latency—Delay between audio input and output. Also used when referring to timing differences between audio tracks and/or audio and midi tracks.

Ltc—Short for Longitudinal Time Code—Synchronization signal for video links that is recorded to a video tape along with images (⇨Vitc).

Mainboard—Basic backbone of the computer on which the ⇨Cpu, memory modules and expansion cards reside.

Midi—Short for ›Musical Instrument Digital Interface;‹ Midi enables synthesizers, sequencers, computers, rhythm machines, etc. to be interconnected through a standard interface and exchange music related data such as notes controller messages, clock and sounds. Midi dictates a uniform data format and connector standard for all manufacturers.

Non-destructive—›Non-destructive audio processing‹ means that the actual audio data in an ⇨audio file is not edited, only peripheral or playback parameters such as ⇨regions and segments/fades etc.

Pci—Short for ›Peripheral Component Interface;‹ Macintosh ⇨Bus standard. Currently the best standard for expansion cards.

Phase—Also called phase position or phase angle; specified in 0 to 360. It describes an attribute of an oscillation that is especially significant when signals overlap.

Plug-in—Modular expansion software that enhances the capabilities of a host program. The internal effects in Lam can be upgraded with third-party plug-ins (also ⇨Vst, ⇨Premiere and ⇨Audiosuite).

PowerMacintosh—General term for Apple Macintosh computer equipped with Ppc processors, including the G3 (Ppc 750 processor) e.g. ›603e‹ or ›604‹ as opposed to the older generation of ›68k‹ processors.

Ppq—Short for ›Pulses Per Quarter;‹ determines how many increments a quarter note is divided into; essential for sequencer timing, among others.

Premiere—Plug-in effect format. Non-realtime and destructive in Lam's Sample Edit window.

Quantize—Corrects poorly timed playing by repositioning events according to a given note grid (e.g. 16th).

Ram—Short for ›Random Access Memory.‹ This is the memory that handles your working data; its capacity is expressed in Mb (megabyte). Normally this memory is ›volatile,‹ which means that the contents are only saved for as long as the device is powered up.

Routing—Generally refers to how a signal is sent through signal circuits; is often used to describe specific input and output ›assignments.‹

Sampling—General term for conversion of analog to digital audio data. Tiny ›samples‹ are taken of an analog waveshape at regular intervals, whereby each sample represents a specific numeric value. These numeric values constitute the digital audio data stream.

Sample rate—Also called sampling frequency. The term describes the frequency at which audio material is sampled, processed or played back.

Sample rate converter—Device or algorithm that translates one ⇨sample rate into another.

Scsi—Short for ›Small Computer Systems Interface;‹ a hardware interface and data bus which allows the connection of peripheral devices such as hard disks, Cd-Roms and scanners to a computer.

Simm—Short for ›Single In-line Memory Module;‹ board with ⇨Ram modules that is plugged into the corresponding ⇨slots on the computer's mainboard.

Slot—General term for expansion ports on the computer's mainboard. Either Nubus or Pci.

S/P-Dif—Short for ›**S**ony/**P**hilips **D**igital **I**nter**F**ace;‹ standard format for transporting digital audio data. Consumer version of ⇨Aes/Ebu.

Synchronization—General term for timing between audio and Midi tracks within Logic Audio and also for timing information passed between Logic and external devices such as drum and tape machines or external sequencers.

System Extension—Files required by the Mac Os so that it can address expansion components such as hard disks, Midi interfaces or soundcards. System extensions also add functionality to the Mac Os allowing for things like; access to various file types and other enhancements.

Tdif—Short for ›**T**ascam **D**igital **I**nterface **F**ormat;‹ a digital 8-channel interface that is primarily used for connecting digital multi-track recorder (Dtr) by Tascam.

Terminator—In a ⇨Scsi Bus, the first and last device in the chain have to be equipped with an activated terminating resistor, the circumspectly-named ›terminator.‹ Available either as a software switch or external plug that fits the Scsi port.

Track At Once—⇨Cd-R recorder mode: Each track is written individually to the ⇨Cd-R. ⇨Disk At Once.

Transients—Extremely brief signal peaks, for instance a kick drum impulse with a great deal of ›click.‹

Ultra-ATA—Is an updated version of EIDE which allows higher speed data transfers between hard disks/CD-ROMS and the computer.

USB—Short for ›Universal Serial Bus;‹ a hardware connection/bus found on modern computers. Allows data transmission of up to 12 MBit/sec and devices (such as hard/floppy disks, scanners, digital cameras, MIDI interfaces etc.) can be connected/disconnected while the computer is running without the need to reboot.

VITC—Short for Vertically Integrated Time Code; synchronization signal for video interfacing; it is blended into the video signal. In contrast to LTC, the synchronization signal can also be read in a static image. Supported by Unitor8.

VST—A free package of software interfaces for developers (⇨API). It was developed by Steinberg to be used as a plug-in interface to Cubase VST. It is also used in LAM's ⇨plug-in architecture.

Word Clock—Clock signal at ⇨sample rate frequency, used by digital audio devices to ensure they run in absolute sync.

WORM—Short for ›Write Once Read Many‹ is the way CD-Recorders write data to a blank CD i.e. it can only be written to once, but read multiple times.

And This Year's WIZOO Winners Are ...

The winner of the Dalai Lama ultimate karma award goes to Ralf Kleinermanns whose source material provided not only a structure, but indeed some of the body to both the book and CD-ROM.

Peter Gorges for his massive assistance and direction with the guide and, on the lighter side, poodle training, that ›one drink too many,‹ tasteful magazine design and Kraftwerk at Warp 9.

Andreas Dedring, Thorsten Adam, Clemens Homburg, Gerhard Lengeling and the rest of the team at Emagic for their creativity, support and assistance

And from:

Arboretum Systems—Todd Souvignier

dB audioware—Dave Brown

Tc Works—Ralf Schluenzen

Waves—Mitch Thomas

Guys and gals, your support has been invaluable.

Dave ›Strawberry‹ Field, Nick Dafilis and the gang from the Electric Factory in Australia.

Michael, Laura and Max Allen (his first credit). Thanks for the pearls of wisdom ... and endless absurdity ... over the years.

And lastly, my wife Sharon and best friends Peter and Julie for their support and patience with me.

›Ho!‹

Index

Numbers

A

D

E

Wizoo Books and Cd-Roms

On the following pages, you'll find an excerpt from our growing book and Cd-Rom catalog.

Be sure to check out the latest updates to the book and Cd-Rom program at our Web site at `http://www.wizoo.com/`

Feel free to order any of the wonderful Wizoo products via the coupon at the end of the book by credit card.

All Wizoo Books are available in English and German versions.

More Wizoo Books for Logic Users

Peter Gorges/Ralf Kleinermanns:

Logic Audio Fx Collection

- 500 professional presets for the internal plug-ins

Make the most of Logic 4's effects! Featuring 500 professional plug & play presets for all application areas: signal processing, arrangement, sound design, mixing and mastering. Plus a brief description of and tips-n-tricks for each preset.

- For Logic Audio Silver, Gold and Platinum, Macintosh and Windows, Version 4 and higher.

Order no.	Isbn
WizLH00013E	3-927954-52-7

Peter Gorges: **Logic Audio from A to Z**

► Look it up. Understand it. Drive on.

This WIZOO reference book should never be more than an arm's length away from every Logic Audio system. Every function, menu item, parameter and key command in Logic Audio is explained clearly and concisely-short, sweet and to the point. Ordered alphabetically and by functional area, you'll immediately find what you're looking for. This book is the definitive place to the fastest help whenever you're stuck or simply want to learn more about Logic Audio.

► For Logic Silver, Gold and Platinum, Macintosh and Windows. Available fall 1999.

Order no.	ISBN
WIZLH00016E	3-927954-58-6

Dave Bellingham: **Logic Audio Windows**

► Faster, more effective and creative production

Windows version of the WIZOO Guide Logic Audio Macintosh. Tailored to Windows and featuring a special hard- and software guide for Windows computers.

► And of course an included CD-ROM featuring audio and song files, shareware, demos and utilities.

Order no.	ISBN
WIZLH00008E	3-927954-47-0

Other WIZOO Books

		Order No	ISBN	US $
WIZOO Basics				
Reinhard Schmitz	Analog Synthesis	WIZBA00001E	3-927954-37-3	29.95
Claudius Brüse	Music and Computers	WIZBA00002E	3-927954-43-8	29.95
Clemens Kurtz	Sequening with Cubase	WIZBA00005E	3-927954-54-3	29,95
WIZOO Guides				
Dave Bellingham/ Peter Gorges	Kawai K-5000	WIZLH00001E	3-927954-21-7	29.95
Peter Gorges	Nord Modular	WIZLH00002E	3-927954-23-3	29.95
Udo Weyers	Roland JV/XP	WIZLH00003E	3-927954-25-X	29.95
Ralf Kleinermanns	Cubase VST Windows	WIZLH00004E	3-927954-27-6	29.95
René Algesheimer	Top 30 Music Shareware Windows	WIZLH00005E	3-927954-29-2	29.95
Ralf Kleinermanns	Cubase VST Plug-Ins	WIZLH00007E	3-927954-33-0	34.95
Ralf Kleinermanns	Cubase VST Macintosh	WIZLH00010E	3-927954-49-7	29.95
Thomas Adam	WIZOO Guide FX	WIZLH00006E	3-927954-31-4	29.95
Dave Bellingham	Logic Audio Windows	WIZLH00008E	3-927954-47-0	29.95
Dave Bellingham	Logic Audio Macintosh	WIZLH00011E	3-927954-50-0	29.95
Peter Gorges/ Ralf Kleinermanns	Logic Audio FX Collection	WIZLH00013E	3-927954-52-7	49.90
Peter Gorges	Logic Audio from A to Z	WIZLH00016E	3-927954-58-6	49.90
WIZOO Pro Guides				
Len Sasso	MetaSynth 2.5	WIZLH00012E	3-927954-45-4	34.95
Jörg Sunderkötter	Groove Programming in Cubase VST	WIZLH00009E	3-927954-35-7	34.95

Wizoo CD-Roms

Programmer	Title	Order No.	Format	Us $
Claudius Brüse/ PeterGorges	T-Rex	Wizsc00001C	Akai S1000	49.95
		Wizsc00001P	Aiff/Wav/SoundFont	44.95
Michael Mühlhaus/ Bernhard Reiss	Hamburg Loopz	Wizsc00002C	Akai S1000	49.95
		Wizsc00002P	Aiff/Wav/B. Box	29.95
Frank Heiss/Dr.Walker	LoFi Junkiez Vol. 1	Wizsc00003C	Akai S1000	49.95
		Wizsc00003P	Aiff/Wav	29.95
Johannes Waehneldt	Magnetica	Wizsc00004C	Akai S3000/5000/6000	49.95
		Wizsc00004E	Emu E IV	49.95
Peter Gorges	Wizoo powered Wave	Wizsc00005C	Akai S3000/5000/6000	49.95
Peter Gorges	Wizoo powered Nord	Wizsc00006C	Akai S3000/5000/6000	49.95
Peter Gorges	Wizoo powered Dx	Wizsc00007C	Akai S3000/5000/6000	49.95
Michael Mühlhaus / Christian Obermaier	Hamburg Loopz Vol. II	Wizsc00009P	Wav/Audio	49.95
Frank Heiss/Dr.Walker	LoFi Junkiez Vol. II	Wizsc00010P	Wav/Audio	49.95
Leschet/Schmitz/Dr. Walker/Flux/Digital	Cologne Cyclez	Wizcc00001V	2-Vinyl Set	21.95
Leschet/Schmitz/Dr. Walker/Flux/Digital	Cologne Cyclez I & II	Wizcc00001A	Wav/Audio	49.95

This is how you order:

Online
Visit our Web site
`http://www.wizoo.com/`
At Wizoo, you can fill up your online shopping cart with goodies such as books and CD-ROMs and order them via credit card, fax or email.

European countries
Wizoo
An der Wachsfabrik 8
D-50996 Cologne
Germany

Phone
+49 2236 96217-25

Fax
+49 2236 96217-5

Email
`shoporder@wizoo.com`

Other countries
Wizoo Usa
c/o Music Trade Center
495 Lorimer Street
Brooklyn NY 11211

Toll-free phone
+1-800-579-4832

Fax
+1-718-302-4890

Email
`shoporder_usa@wizoo.com`

(: wizoo :)

Item No.	Item	Quantity	Price
		Shipping	
		SUM	

Credit card VISA ( ) American Express ( ) Eurocard ( )
valid thru (: :) Cardholder (: :)
Card Number (: :)

Last Name/Name

Street No./Street Name

Suburb/Town & ZIP

State/Region & Country

Telephone

Date/Signature

Shipping and Handling
European Countries: Add 4.00 DM (2.50 US $) for each item, orders over 100.00 DM (60.00 US $) are shipped free of charge.
Other Countries: Add 8.00 DM (5.00 US $) for each item, orders over 200.00 DM (120.00 US $) are shipped free of charge.